TEACHER'S PET PUBLICATIONS

LITPLAN TEACHER PACK
for
Go Ask Alice
based on the anonymous diary of a teenage girl
Edited by Dr. Beatrice Sparks

Written by
Christina Stone

© 2008 Teacher's Pet Publications
All Rights Reserved

Copyright Teacher's Pet Publications 2008

Only the student materials in this unit plan (such as worksheets, study questions, and tests) may be reproduced multiple times for use in the purchaser's classroom.

For any additional copyright questions, contact Teacher's Pet Publications.

www.tpet.com

TABLE OF CONTENTS - *Go Ask Alice*

Introduction	5
Unit Objectives	7
Reading Assignment Sheet	8
Unit Outline	9
Study Questions (Short Answer)	13
Quiz/Study Questions (Multiple Choice)	24
Pre-reading Vocabulary Worksheets	45
Lesson One (Introductory Lesson)	59
Non-fiction Assignment Sheet	69
Oral Reading Evaluation Form	73
Writing Assignment 1	65
Writing Assignment 2	76
Writing Assignment 3	82
Writing Evaluation Form	66
Vocabulary Review Activities	102
Extra Writing Assignments/Discussion ?s	88
Unit Review Activities	103
Unit Tests	107
Unit Resource Materials	139
Vocabulary Resource Materials	161

A FEW NOTES ABOUT THE EDITOR

Dr. Beatrice Sparks is a Mormon youth counselor and psychologist in Utah. She was born in 1955 in Idaho, and attended both the University of California at Los Angeles and Brigham Young University.

Aside from counseling troubled youth, Dr. Sparks has also worked as a music therapist in the Utah State Mental Hospital and taught courses at her alma mater BYU.

Dr. Sparks has stated in interviews that her work with teenagers has prompted her to collect the diaries of troubled teens to serve as cautionary tales for others. *Go Ask Alice* was the first book she edited, though at the time the book was published she chose not to include her name on the novel. Since then, she has collected and published several other anonymous diaries of teens including *Jay's Journal, It Happened to Nancy, Almost Lost, Annie's Baby, Treacherous Love, Kim: Empty Inside,* and *Finding Katie.*

Many critics question the validity of the diaries as well as Dr. Sparks' credentials. Though many of her novels credit her as "Dr. Beatrice Sparks, PhD," journalists could not confirm when and where she earned her doctorate. Counseling and other professional qualifications are also not documented.

Dr. Sparks frequently contradicts herself in interviews regarding the authenticity of the diary. She states that the diary is true and accurate, claiming that part of Alice's diary was destroyed after transcription, while the other part remains locked in a publisher's vault. In other interviews, she admits that the diary is a compilation of the original text and fictional events based on her counseling sessions with other teens. The truth behind *Go Ask Alice* and Dr. Spark's other published diaries is highly controversial. More information on the matter is easily found on the Internet.

INTRODUCTION

This LitPlan has been designed to develop students' reading, writing, thinking, and language skills through exercises and activities related to *Go Ask Alice*. It includes twenty one lessons, supported by extra resource materials.

The **introductory lesson** introduces students to the title of the book. The author of the diary is anonymous, and the name selected holds a lot of meaning. This activity lets students explore where the title of the novel came from and the meaning it ads to the novel. Following the introductory activity, students are given the materials they will be using during the unit. At the end of the lesson, students begin the pre-reading work for the first reading assignment.

The **reading assignments** are approximately thirty pages each; some are a little shorter while others are a little longer. Students have approximately 15 minutes of pre-reading work to do prior to each reading assignment. This pre-reading work involves reviewing the study questions for the assignment and doing some vocabulary work for 10 vocabulary words they will encounter in their reading.

The **study guide questions** are fact-based questions; students can find the answers to these questions right in the text. These questions come in two formats: short answer or multiple choice. The best use of these materials is probably to use the short answer version of the questions as study guides for students (since answers will be more complete), and to use the multiple choice version for occasional quizzes.

The **vocabulary work** is intended to enrich students' vocabularies as well as to aid in the students' understanding of the book. Prior to each reading assignment, students will complete a two-part worksheet for 10 vocabulary words in the upcoming reading assignment. Part I focuses on students' use of general knowledge and contextual clues by giving the sentence in which the word appears in the text. Students are then to write down what they think the words mean based on the words' usage. Part II nails down the definitions of the words by giving students dictionary definitions of the words and having students match the words to the correct definitions based on the words' contextual usage. Students should then have an understanding of the words when they meet them in the text.

After each reading assignment, students will go back and formulate answers for the study guide questions. Discussion of these questions serves as a **review** of the most important events and ideas presented in the reading assignments.

After students complete reading the work, there is a **vocabulary review** lesson which pulls together all of the fragmented vocabulary lists for the reading assignments and gives students a review of all of the words they have studied.

Following the vocabulary review, a lesson is devoted to the **extra discussion questions/writing assignments**. These questions focus on interpretation, critical analysis, and personal response, employing a variety of thinking skills and adding to the students' understanding of the novel.

There is a **reflective diary project** in this unit. This project requires students to keep a diary and explore how events, communication, and peers affect their lives.

There are three **writing assignments** in this unit, each with the purpose of informing, persuading, or having students express personal opinions. The first writing assignment asks students to analyze the influences their friends have on their own thoughts and actions. The second assignment asks students to persuade a friend to stop using drugs. The third assignment gives students several roles from which to write.

There is a nonfiction **reading assignment**. Students must read nonfiction articles, books, etc. to gather information about their themes in our world today.

The **review lesson** pulls together all of the aspects of the unit. The teacher is given four or five choices of activities or games to use which all serve the same basic function of reviewing all of the information presented in the unit.

The **unit test** comes in two formats: multiple choice or short answer. As a convenience, two different tests for each format have been included. There is also an advanced short answer unit test for advanced students.

There are additional **support materials** included with this unit. The **Unit Resource Materials** section includes suggestions for an in-class library, crossword and word search puzzles related to the novel, and extra worksheets. There is a list of **bulletin board ideas** which gives the teacher suggestions for bulletin boards to go along with this unit. In addition, there is a list of **extra class activities** the teacher could choose from to enhance the unit or as a substitution for an exercise the teacher might feel is inappropriate for his/her class. **Answer keys** are located directly after the **reproducible student materials** throughout the unit. The **Vocabulary Resource Materials** section includes similar worksheets and games to reinforce the vocabulary words.

The **level** of this unit can be varied depending upon the criteria on which the individual assignments are graded, the teacher's expectations of his/her students in class discussions, and the formats chosen for the study guides, quizzes and test. If teachers have other ideas/activities they wish to use, they can usually easily be inserted prior to the review lesson.

The student materials may be reproduced for use in the teacher's classroom without infringement of copyrights. No other portion of this unit may be reproduced without the written consent of Teacher's Pet Publications, Inc.

UNIT OBJECTIVES - *Go Ask Alice*

1. Through reading the anonymous diary *Go Ask Alice*, students will look at the effects of drugs on a teenager's life.

2. Students will demonstrate their understanding of the text on four levels: factual, interpretive, critical and personal.

3. Students will make connections with the material in the text and apply the lessons learned to their lives.

4. Students will be given the opportunity to practice reading aloud and silently to improve their skills in each area.

5. Students will answer questions to demonstrate their knowledge and understanding of the main events and characters in *Go Ask Alice* as they relate to the author's theme development.

6. Students will enrich their vocabularies and improve their understanding of the novel through the vocabulary lessons prepared for use in conjunction with the novel.

7. The writing assignments in this unit are geared to several purposes:
    a. To have students demonstrate their abilities to inform, to persuade, or to express their own personal ideas

    Note: Students will demonstrate ability to write effectively to <u>inform</u> by developing and organizing facts to convey information. Students will demonstrate the ability to write effectively to <u>persuade</u> by selecting and organizing relevant information, establishing an argumentative purpose, and by designing an appropriate strategy for an identified audience. Students will demonstrate the ability to write effectively to <u>express personal ideas</u> by selecting a form and its appropriate elements.
    b. To check the students' reading comprehension
    c. To make students think about the ideas presented by the novel
    d. To encourage logical thinking
    e. To provide an opportunity to practice good grammar and improve students' use of the English language.

8. Students will read aloud, report, and participate in large and small group discussions to improve their public speaking and personal interaction skills.

READING ASSIGNMENT SHEET - *Go Ask Alice*

Date Assigned	Pages Assigned	Completion Date
	Assignment 1 September 16-July 10	
	Assignment 2 July 13-November 16	
	Assignment 3 November 19-End of Diary One	
	Assignment 4 Diary Number Two-July 3	
	Assignment 5 July 7- Epilogue	

UNIT OUTLINE - *Go Ask Alice*

1 Introduction Activity Project Assignment PVR1	2 Study Quest. 1 Review Vocab 1 Time Line PVR2	3 Writing Assignment #1	4 Study Quest. 2 Review Vocab 2 Nonfiction Assignment	5 Poem Assignment PVR3
6 Speaker	7 Study Quest. 3 Review Vocab 3 Oral Reading Evaluation PVR4	8 Study Quest. 4 Review Vocab 4 New Anti-Drug Campaign Activity	9 Writing Assignment #2 PVR5	10 Study Quest. 5 Review Vocab 5 Campaign Groups
11 Daytime Talk Show	12 Writing Assignment #3 Campaign Groups	13 Present Anti-Drug Campaign Date Comparison	14 Movie	15 Movie Cont. Discussion: book vs. movie
16 Censorship Debate	17 Extra Discussion Questions	18 Extra Discussion Quest. Cont. Reflective Diary Due	19 Vocabulary Review	20 Unit Review
21 Unit Test				

Key: P = Preview Study Questions   V = Vocabulary Work   R= Read

STUDY GUIDE QUESTIONS

SHORT ANSWER STUDY GUIDE QUESTIONS – *Go Ask Alice*

Assignment #1
September 16-July 10
1. What did Roger do to Alice that has her so upset?
2. Why is Alice's family moving?
3. Alice says she wants to get all new stuff when she moves. What is the only thing she owns that she would like to keep?
4. How can the reader tell that Alice has an eating disorder?
5. Why does Alice love Christmas?
6. Alice worked hard to pick out a Christmas gift her mother would really love. How did her mother react when she opened the gift?
7. Why is Alice jealous of her brother and sister when it comes to going to school and making friends in a new place?
8. Who are Tim and Alex?
9. How is Alice's first day at her new school?
10. Alice was excited to stay with her grandparents all summer. Why is she suddenly so upset to leave her new home to visit her grandparents?
11. Alice is bored out of her mind at her grandparent's house. What happens that gives Alice something exciting to do?
12. Describe the game "Button, Button, Who's Got the Button."
13. Describe Alice's first high.
14. Alice says she will not try drugs again. Why does she feel this way?

Assignment #2
July 13-November 16
1. Why does Alice need to buy a metal box with a lock?
2. Why does Alice feel obligated to stay with her grandparents and help out?
3. What big step does Alice take with Bill?
4. What is Alice worrying about that is keeping her from sleeping and requiring the doctor to give her sleeping pills and tranquilizers?
5. How do Alice and Roger reconnect with each other?
6. What is Alice most worried about in her relationship with Roger?
7. Alice gets sleeping pills from her doctor, but admits she doesn't really need the sleep. What is it she says she needs instead?
8. Who is Chris?
9. What is Alice's first job?
10. How does Alice get through the long, stressful days of school and work while also dealing with her parents when she gets home?
11. According to Alice's friend, why do more kids prefer drugs to alcohol?
12. Why does Alice decide not to go to college?
13. Alice begins to sell drugs to help her boyfriend earn money. Who does she sell drugs to that makes her feel really guilty and upset?
14. Describe the life Alice and Chris are living in San Francisco.

Go Ask Alice Study Questions page 2

Assignment #3
November 19-End of Diary One
1. After vowing to never do drugs again, Alice and Chris get mixed up in the drug scene in San Francisco. What event prompts the two friends to begin using drugs again?
2. What happens to Alice and Chris that makes them leave San Francisco?
3. Describe the new shop Alice and Chris open near Berkeley.
4. What is Alice's life at home like when she returns from California?
5. What is the best part of the New Year's Eve party Alice's parents throw?
6. How do other students react when Alice returns to school?
7. Alice confides to her mom that kids at school are pressuring her to use drugs. What do her parents do to provide additional support?
8. Why does Alice have to see a shrink?
9. What is Alice's situation at home like when she decides to run away again?
10. When Alice runs away a second time, she continues writing but not in her diary. What does she use instead?
11. What are the three places Alice lives when she runs away for a second time?
12. Where does Alice sleep when she runs away for a second time?
13. What do the people at the mission do for Alice?
14. How does Alice get money to buy drugs?
15. Alice is worried that with all the sex she is having she may get pregnant. Why can't she take the birth control pill to protect herself?
16. Why does Alice want to get a new diary when she gets back home?
17. What career path does Alice decide to take when she graduates from high school?

Assignment #4
Diary Number Two-July 3
1. How does Alice perform as a student when she returns to school?
2. What special act does Alice do for her mother's birthday?
3. How can the reader tell the kids at school don't believe that Alice is really through with drugs?
4. What type of file does Alice start that will help her with her goal of becoming a counselor?
5. When Alice's grandpa dies, she has morbid thoughts and nightmares about him. What does she dwell on about death in these thoughts and nightmares?
6. How does Alice meet Joel?
7. How does Joel fit in with Alice and her family?
8. What happened while Alice was babysitting for Mrs. Larsen?
9. What do the kids at school threaten to do to Alice's family?
10. What do the kids at school do to Alice to try and get her in trouble with the principal?
11. What happens to Alice as she is taking a walk in the park?
12. What do Joel and Alice exchange as symbols of their relationship before he leaves to go home for the summer?
13. What happened to Chris?

Go Ask Alice Study Questions page 3

Assignment #5
<u>July 7- Epilogue</u>
1. Why does Mrs. Larsen need Alice to babysit, cook, and clean for her?
2. Describe the physical condition Alice is in at the hospital.
3. How did Alice end up on the bad acid trip that landed her in the hospital?
4. Describe the hallucination Alice had while on a bad acid trip and how the hallucination correlates with her injuries.
5. Alice claims she did not take the drugs on purpose and was tricked. Knowing her history of drugs and running away, what do Alice's parents think?
6. Alice's case is heard before the court to determine what will happen to her when she is released from the hospital. Aside from the previous drug charge on her record, what other evidence is presented to the judge to make him rule against Alice?
7. When Alice finds out she is going to be placed in the state mental hospital, how does she feel?
8. The youth section of the mental hospital classifies patients into Group One and Group Two. What is the difference between these two groups?
9. Why does Alice begin interviewing the other patients at the hospital?
10. Alice becomes friends with a young girl named Babbie while staying at the hospital. What surprising news does Alice discover about Babbie's parents?
11. Who writes Alice a ten page letter while she is in the hospital? What does the letter say?
12. When Alice gets back home she begins to pray. Aside from herself, who does she ask God to help?
13. Why do Alice and her family take a trip to the east coast for a couple weeks?
14. Who is Fawn?
15. Why does Alice's piano teacher call?
16. What does Alice's family do for her birthday?
17. What happens after Alice decides not to keep a diary?

ANSWER KEY SHORT ANSWER STUDY GUIDE QUESTIONS – *Go Ask Alice*

Assignment #1
September 16-July 10

1. What did Roger do to Alice that has her so upset?
   Roger asked Alice out on a date and never showed up.

2. Why is Alice's family moving?
   Her father got a better job in another state. He will be the Dean of Political Science at a university.

3. Alice says she wants to get all new stuff when she moves. What is the only thing she owns that she would like to keep?
   Alice says that she would never want to get rid of her books since they are a part of her.

4. How can the reader tell that Alice has an eating disorder?
   Alice skips meals, is obsessed with losing weight, is getting sick, and mentions making herself throw up. Her mother comments that she is getting too thin and won't allow her to diet anymore.

5. Why does Alice love Christmas?
   Alice loves Christmas because she is surrounded by family and feels "warm and secure and needed and wanted."

6. Alice worked hard to pick out a Christmas gift her mother would really love. How did her mother react when she opened the gift?
   Alice's mother was thrilled to get the pearl pin. She put it on her nightgown and wore it all day.

7. Why is Alice jealous of her brother and sister when it comes to going to school and making friends in a new place?
   Alice's brother met a boy from down the street and made friends even before school started. She is jealous because he will have a friend when he starts school. Alice's sister will be going to school with the daughter of someone her father works with, so she will have a friend at the start of school too.

8. Who are Tim and Alex?
   Tim is Alice's younger brother, and Alex (Alexandria) is Alice's little sister.

9. How is Alice's first day at her new school?
   No one talked to her all day. During lunch Alice said she was sick so she didn't have to eat alone and she skipped her last class to go pig out on junk food.

10. Alice was excited to stay with her grandparents all summer. Why is she suddenly so upset to leave her new home to visit her grandparents?
    Alice has met a girl named Beth who has become her best friend. The two are very close and don't want to be separated all summer.

11. Alice is bored out of her mind at her grandparent's house. What happens that gives Alice something exciting to do?
    Alice runs into Jill, a popular girl from her old school, and get invited to a party.

12. Describe the game "Button, Button, Who's Got the Button."
    In this game a tray of fourteen sodas is brought out. Ten of the drinks contain the drug LSD. Ten "lucky" people get high, while the others babysit.

13. Describe Alice's first high.
    Alice loses all her inhibitions. She experiences every sound, touch, and sight to the fullest. She really loves the feeling she has when high and feels happier and more carefree than ever before.

14. Alice says she will not try drugs again. Why does she feel this way?
    Alice has heard too many bad stories about people on drugs. She enjoyed it when it was given to her without her knowledge, but doesn't want to end up like the people she has heard about.

Assignment #2
July 13-November 16
1. Why does Alice need to buy a metal box with a lock?
    Alice needs a safe place to put her diary since she has been talking about her drug use so openly. She wants to buy a metal box with a lock so no one will be able to read her diary.

2. Why does Alice feel obligated to stay with her grandparents and help out?
    Alice's grandfather had a heart attack and she feels like she should help out around the house so that her grandmother can spend her time helping her grandfather recover.

3. What big step does Alice take with Bill?
    Alice loses her virginity to Bill one night when they are high.

4. What is Alice worrying about that is keeping her from sleeping and requiring the doctor to give her sleeping pills and tranquilizers?
    Alice is worried she might be pregnant from having unprotected sex with Bill.

5. How do Alice and Roger reconnect with each other?
    Roger and his family stop by Alice's grandparents house since they heard her grandfather had a heart attack.

6. What is Alice most worried about in her relationship with Roger?
   Alice is terrified that Roger will find out about her recent drug use and sexual encounter.

7. Alice gets sleeping pills from her doctor, but admits she doesn't really need the sleep. What is it she says she needs instead?
   Alice needs an escape from her life and the sleeping pills allow her to have that.

8. Who is Chris?
   Chris is a girl Alice met at a local clothing boutique. The two hit it off and have become friends.

9. What is Alice's first job?
   Alice gets a job working at the clothing boutique with Chris.

10. How does Alice get through the long, stressful days of school and work while also dealing with her parents when she gets home?
    Alice has to take drugs to keep her alert and high at school and in social situations and then tranquilizers to mellow out when she gets home.

11. According to Alice's friend, why do more kids prefer drugs to alcohol?
    Alice's friend says that drugs are easier for teenagers to get than alcohol.

12. Why does Alice decide not to go to college?
    Alice feels like her boyfriend, Richie, needs her help. She decides not to go to college so she can help him earn money to pay for his medical degree.

13. Alice begins to sell drugs to help her boyfriend earn money. Who does she sell drugs to that makes her feel really guilty and upset?
    Alice feels bad for selling drugs to elementary school students.

14. Describe the life Alice and Chris are living in San Francisco.
    Alice and Chris are living in small, dirty apartment and are having trouble finding jobs. They both work very hard all day long and are living life very differently than they expected.

Assignment #3
November 19-End of Diary One

1. After vowing to never do drugs again, Alice and Chris get mixed up in the drug scene in San Francisco. What event prompts the two friends to begin using drugs again?
   Chris's boss, Shelia, invites the girls to a party at her house. Alice and Chris go to the party to find that people are passing around a joint. The girls can't resist and begin heavy drug use once again.

2. What happens to Alice and Chris that makes them leave San Francisco?
   Alice and Chris are raped by Shelia and her boyfriend while high one night.

3. Describe the new shop Alice and Chris open near Berkeley.
    Alice and Chris open a shop where college kids stop by to watch TV and sit around. There is a regular crowd and the business is fairly successful.

4. What is Alice's life at home like when she returns from California?
    Alice is welcomed home by her entire family. They all cry and are happy to see her. It is Christmas and Alice appreciates every moment with her family. They seem to get along with no problems and are just happy to be reunited.

5. What is the best part of the New Year's Eve party Alice's parents throw?
    After all the guests leave, Alice and her family put on the their pajamas and clean up the mess. The family laughs and goofs off, having fun together naturally. This is Alice's favorite part of the whole party.

6. How do other students react when Alice returns to school?
    Several kids approach Alice and harass her for drugs. She used to sell drugs and they don't believe that she has changed. Many of Alice's old friends try to get her to go to parties and be the person she was before she left.

7. Alice confides to her mom that kids at school are pressuring her to use drugs. What do her parents do to provide additional support?
    Alice's parents try to plan fun activities for Alice and Chris over the weekends to keep them occupied and away from drugs. Her mother also screens phone calls of people who Alice wants to avoid.

8. Why does Alice have to see a shrink?
    Chris's house gets raided by the police one night while Chris and Alice are high. Since it is her first offense, Alice's parents make a bargain with the court to send her to a psychologist instead of going to court.

9. What is Alice's situation at home like when she decides to run away again?
    Alice's parents have her on probation. They watch everything she does and she can't talk to any of her friends or do anything without her parent's supervision.

10. When Alice runs away a second time, she continues writing but not in her diary. What does she use instead?
    Alice uses single sheets of paper, paper bags, and other items around her to write her diary entries.

11. What are the three places Alice lives when she runs away for a second time?
    Alice lives in Denver, Colorado; Coos Bay, Oregon; Southern California.

12. Where does Alice sleep when she runs away for a second time?
    Alice shares a place with other drugs users and sometimes sleeps in the park.

13. What do the people at the mission do for Alice?
    The people at the mission let Alice take a shower and give her some clean clothes and tampons. They feed her and take her to the doctor for her fever and try to talk to her about communicating with her parents.

14. How does Alice get money to buy drugs?
    Alice panhandles on the side of the road, begging people for money. She also performs sexual favors with strangers to get drugs.

15. Alice is worried that with all the sex she is having she may get pregnant. Why can't she take the birth control pill to protect herself?
    Alice uses so many drugs and blacks out so often that she can rarely tell what day it is. She can't take the pill for protection unless she can remember to take it each day, so she just hopes she doesn't end up pregnant.

16. Why does Alice want to get a new diary when she gets back home?
    Alice feels like her first diary is her past, her life on drugs. When she gets home she wants to start a new diary that will be her future, a life without drugs.

17. What career path does Alice decide to take when she graduates from high school?
    Alice decides to become a child guidance counselor or a psychologist so that she can help others in her same situation.

Assignment #4
Diary Number Two-July 3
1. How does Alice perform as a student when she returns to school?
   Alice becomes a very devoted student. She studies for several hours each night and gets very high grades in all her classes.

2. What special act does Alice do for her mother's birthday?
   Alice cooks an entire meal all by herself as a surprise for her mother's birthday.

3. How can the reader tell the kids at school don't believe that Alice is really through with drugs?
   The kids involved in drugs still ask her to parties and the straight kids won't talk to her because they still consider her to be a druggie.

4. What type of file does Alice start that will help her with her goal of becoming a counselor?
   Alice starts to collect statistics relating to kids and drugs to keep for when she becomes a counselor.

5. When Alice's grandpa dies, she has morbid thoughts and nightmares about him. What does she dwell on about death in these thoughts and nightmares?
   Alice thinks about the decay of her grandpa's body, envisioning him with worms and maggots eating away at his body.

6. How does Alice meet Joel?
    Alice's dad gets special permission for her to use the university library. While she is there studying one afternoon she meets Joel, a student at the university.

7. How does Joel fit in with Alice and her family?
    Joel feels comfortable having dinners with the family and long discussions with her father. He seems to get along well with everyone in the family and shows Alice a lot of respect.

8. What happened while Alice was babysitting for Mrs. Larsen?
    Jan, an old friend from when Alice did drugs, stopped by and said she wanted to babysit because she needed the money. Jan was obviously stoned and Alice was concerned about the safety of the baby and so she called Jan's mother to come get her.

9. What do the kids at school threaten to do to Alice's family?
    The kids at school say they will get even for her calling Jan's mother. They threaten to give Alice's younger brother and sister candy laced with drugs. They also threaten to put drugs in her father's car to make him look bad and lose his job.

10. What do the kids at school do to Alice to try and get her in trouble with the principal?
    Someone places a burning roach in her locker, trying to make it look like she had drugs with her at school so she would get in trouble.

11. What happens to Alice as she is taking a walk in the park?
    A guy Alice doesn't even know grabs her by the arm and threatens her for being a fink. He then takes her behind the bushes and kisses her, threatening to do more.

12. What do Joel and Alice exchange as symbols of their relationship before he leaves to go home for the summer?
    Joel gives Alice a gold watch his father had given him and Alice gives Joel a ring that belonged to her grandmother.

13. What happened to Chris?
    Chris's parents moved her to a town where no one knew about her past.

Assignment #5
<u>July 7- Epilogue</u>
1. Why does Mrs. Larsen need Alice to babysit, cook, and clean for her?
    Mrs. Larsen broke her leg in a car accident and she needs someone to take care of the house, her baby, and her husband.

2. Describe the physical condition Alice is in at the hospital.
    Alice has torn off the tops of her fingers, she has missing fingernails, her face is scratched and clawed up, she is missing chunks of her hair and her scalp is exposed, her body is badly bruised, and several of her toes are broken. She also has a brain concussion.

3. How did Alice end up on the bad acid trip that landed her in the hospital?
   One of the kids from school who was angry at Alice for snitching put acid on some chocolate covered peanuts and left them on the counter while Alice was babysitting. Alice thought they were a gift for her from Mr. Larsen and didn't know they were coated in acid.

4. Describe the hallucination Alice had while on a bad acid trip and how the hallucination correlates with her injuries.
   Alice sees her grandfather covered in worms, maggots, and parasites and imagines them multiplying all over the house and covering her body. She feels them eating her fleshing and consuming every part of her body. She then imagines being forced into a casket and trying to scream and claw her way out. Since Alice is imagining worms all over her, she is trying to rip them off, but is really just ripping off pieces of her skin and chunks of hair. A neighbor hears Alice going crazy and comes over, locking her in a small closet until help gets there. This is where Alice thought she was being shoved into a coffin and is really using her fingers to claw her way out of the closet. This explains the severe damage done to her fingers.

5. Alice claims she did not take the drugs on purpose and was tricked. Knowing her history of drugs and running away, what do Alice's parents think?
   Alice's parents believe Alice was tricked into the acid trip. They believe her when she tells them she had no idea the peanuts left out were coated in acid.

6. Alice's case is heard before the court to determine what will happen to her when she is released from the hospital. Aside from the previous drug charge on her record, what other evidence is presented to the judge to make him rule against Alice?
   Marcie and Jan both lie to the judge and testify that Alice had been trying to sell them drugs for weeks. They both tell the judge that Alice is known around school for selling and using drugs.

7. When Alice finds out she is going to be placed in the state mental hospital, how does she feel?
   Alice is terrified of being placed in a mental hospital. She thinks it is a place for crazy people and is scared. She doesn't feel like she belongs there.

8. The youth section of the mental hospital classifies patients into Group One and Group Two. What is the difference between these two groups?
   Group One kids are on their best behavior and trying to be released. They are the kids who have proved themselves in therapy and in their day to day behavior and because of their actions, have earned special privileges. They get to take trips out of the hospital and have all the privileges one can earn in the hospital. The Group Two kids are basically on probation. They haven't been obeying the rules and don't get any special privileges.

9. Why does Alice begin interviewing the other patients at the hospital?
   Alice tells her doctor she want so be a social worker. He tells her that she should ask others for their story so that she can better understand what everyone else has been through.

10. Alice becomes friends with a young girl named Babbie while staying at the hospital. What surprising news does Alice discover about Babbie's parents?
    Alice finds out that Babbie's parents don't want her anymore. She has been too much trouble and they want her to live with a foster family instead of coming home.

11. Who writes Alice a ten page letter while she is in the hospital? What does the letter say?
    Joel writes Alice a letter where he tells her that he knows about her past. He still wants to be with her and understands and forgives her for everything.

12. When Alice gets back home she begins to pray. Aside from herself, who does she ask God to help?
    Alice asks God to help Marcie and Jan get better too.

13. Why do Alice and her family take a trip to the east coast for a couple weeks?
    Alice's father has the chance to fill in for a professor across the country. The family goes with him and makes a little vacation out of it while her father is at work.

14. Who is Fawn?
    Fawn is one of the "straight kids" from school. She asks Alice to come swimming at her house and from there the two become very close friends.

15. Why does Alice's piano teacher call?
    Her piano teacher wants her to be a soloist in an upcoming concert. She wants to use Alice's picture on the program as well.

16. What does Alice's family do for her birthday?
    Alice's family surprises her with a little party. The main part of the surprise is that they had Joel come without Alice knowing until she came down for the party.

17. What happens after Alice decides not to keep a diary?
    Three weeks after Alice stops keeping a diary she is found dead from an overdose on drugs. No one knows whether or not it was accidently or premeditated.

STUDY GUIDE/QUIZ QUESTIONS - *Go Ask Alice*
Multiple Choice Format

Assignment #1
September 16-July 10

1. What did Roger do to Alice that has her so upset?
    A. Roger told the whole school that Alice has never kissed anyone.
    B. Roger asked Alice out on a date and never showed up.
    C. Roger made fun of Alice at lunch and now the whole school makes fun of her.
    D. Roger broke up with Alice on their one-year anniversary.

2. Why is Alice's family moving?
    A. Alice's parents are worried there is too much crime in their city. They are moving to a smaller, safer town.
    B. Alice's parents are getting a divorce. They are moving so her mom and dad can each have their own house, but still be close enough for the kids to visit each parent.
    C. Alice's grandfather is very sick. They are moving to be closer to him so her mother can take care of him.
    D. Alice's father got a better job in another state. He will be the Dean of Political Science at a university.

3. Alice says she wants to get all new stuff when she moves. What is the only thing she owns that she would like to keep?
    A. Her cat
    B. Her clothes
    C. Her books
    D. Her bed

4. How can the reader tell that Alice has an eating disorder?
    A. She is being sent to a psychiatrist to help her deal with her eating problems.
    B. She passed out during school. She hit her head on a desk and had to get stitches.
    C. She writes in her diary a record of how many calories she eats each day and how many she burned from working out. She is keeping a chart of her weight loss.
    D. She skips meals, is obsessed with losing weight, is getting sick, and mentions making herself throw up.

5. Why does Alice love Christmas?
    A. It is the one time of the year she feels warm, secure, needed, and wanted.
    B. She loves getting to see her extended family. She only sees them once a year and it is always a blast.
    C. It is the coldest and darkest part of the year. She feels this type of weather best suits her mood.
    D. She loves getting gifts and seeing the faces of others as she gives them gifts.

Go Ask Alice Multiple Choice Questions for Assignment 1 page 2

6. Alice worked hard to pick out a Christmas gift her mother would really love. How did her mother react when she opened the gift?
    A. She faked a smile and said she liked it, but Alice could tell she was lying.
    B. She was thrilled with her pearl pin. She put it on her nightgown and wore it all day.
    C. She laughed because she bought Alice the same pearl pin.
    D. She asked if she could exchange it for a pair of earrings she liked better.

7. Why is Alice jealous of her brother and sister when it comes to going to school and making friends in a new place?
    A. The only high school in the town is an hour away. She hates having to ride the bus for so long and wishes her school was closer to home like her brother and sister's schools are.
    B. Alice is jealous they aren't in high school. She wishes she was younger so the work wouldn't be so hard.
    C. Alice is jealous because her brother has already met a boy who lives down the street and her sister will be starting school with the daughter of a local professor.
    D. Her brother and sister are really outgoing and will make friends easily while Alice is shy and will have a hard time finding someone to talk to.

8. Who are Tim and Alex?
    A. Alice's younger brother and sister
    B. The two boys who took Alice and Beth out on a double date to the movies
    C. Two boys that Alice dated at her old school
    D. Alice's old best friends who she misses

9. How is Alice's first day at her new school?
    A. She finds out she is very far behind in all her classes since this school moves through the work a lot quicker than her old school.
    B. No one talked to her all day. During lunch Alice said she was sick so she didn't have to eat alone and she skipped her last class to go pig out on junk food.
    C. A group of girls talked to her and invited her to a party. She was excited to be in the new town, now that she had friends.
    D. She does well in her PE class and the coach recruits her for the basketball team.

10. Alice was excited to stay with her grandparents all summer. Why is she suddenly so upset to leave her new home to visit her grandparents?
    A. She finally has a boyfriend in her new town and can't stand to be away from him for that long.
    B. She heard Roger will be working for her grandfather and she will have to see him every day.
    C. She has gained weight and is embarrassed for her old friends to see her that way.
    D. She doesn't want to be separated from her new best friend, Beth.

Go Ask Alice Multiple Choice Questions for Assignment 1 page 3

11. Alice is bored out of her mind at her grandparent's house. What happens that gives Alice something exciting to do?
    A. Roger asks her out on a date.
    B. Jill asks her to go to a party.
    C. Her grandparents teacher her how to drive.
    D. She finds an adorable puppy and gets to keep it.

12. Describe the game "Button, Button, Who's Got the Button."
    A. A tray of fourteen sodas is brought out. Ten of the drinks contain the drug LSD and the point is to figure out who got lucky with the drink laced with drugs.
    B. Music plays as kids pass a button around the circle. When the music stops the person who has the button has to kiss the person to his/her right.
    C. LSD is put on the bottom of a button. The button is put in a basket with pennies. Each person takes one item from the basket and the person with the button gets high.
    D. The numbers one through eight are placed in a basket. Someone draws a number and if there is a person wearing exactly that many buttons, they get to have the LSD.

13. Describe Alice's first high.
    A. Alice loses all her inhibitions and feels happy and carefree.
    B. Alice gets very sick and starts to throw up.
    C. Alice can't remember anything that happened that night.
    D. Alice was scared from the hallucinations and was hoping it would end soon.

14. Alice says she will not try drugs again. Why does she feel this way?
    A. Alice got sicker than she has ever been in her life and never wants to feel that way again.
    B. Alice knows her family has a history of drug abuse and is worried she may become addicted if she tries drugs again.
    C. Alice has heard too many bad stories about people on drugs and doesn't want to end up like them.
    D. Alice knows that she will do things she doesn't want to do if she takes drugs, so in order to maintain her morals, she wants to stay away from drugs.

Go Ask Alice Multiple Choice Questions for Assignment 2

Assignment #2
<u>July 13-November 16</u>
1. Why does Alice need to buy a metal box with a lock?
    A. For a place to hide her stash of drugs
    B. For a place to hide her diary
    C. For a place to hide extra money to buy drugs
    D. For a place to keep all her letters from Roger

2. Why does Alice feel obligated to stay with her grandparents and help out?
    A. Alice knows her grandparents won't be alive for much longer and since she lives so far away she wants to try to spend as much time with them as she can.
    B. Alice's family has been struggling with money since they moved. She feels like if she stays with her grandparents a while longer she will be one less mouth to feed.
    C. Alice started a relationship with Roger and knows that if she wants it to last she needs to stay with her grandparents longer so she can spend more time with Roger.
    D. Alice's grandfather had a heart attack and she feels like she should help out around the house so that her grandmother can spend her time helping her grandfather recover.

3. What big step does Alice take with Bill?
    A. Getting drunk for the first time
    B. Having sex for the first time
    C. Selling drugs for the first time
    D. Getting arrested for the first time

4. What is Alice worrying about that is keeping her from sleeping and requiring the doctor to give her sleeping pills and tranquilizers?
    A. She might be pregnant
    B. Her parents might know she has been using drugs
    C. She might get arrested if the police find out she has been selling drugs
    D. She will not see Roger again after he goes to military school

5. How do Alice and Roger reconnect with each other?
    A. Roger is at Jill's party and discovers that Alice is cooler than he originally thought.
    B. Roger graduated from high school a year early and ended up going to the same school where Alice's dad works.
    C. Roger and his family stop by Alice's grandparents house since they heard her grandfather had a heart attack.
    D. Roger's military school is in San Francisco where he meets up with Alice and Chris after they run away from home.

Go Ask Alice Multiple Choice Questions for Assignment 2 page 2

6. What is Alice most worried about in her relationship with Roger?
    A. Alice is nervous that Roger will hate her family and not want to date her anymore.
    B. Alice is scared Roger will dump her when she goes back home and they can't see each other as often.
    C. Alice is worried Roger will go to military school and find another girl he likes better than her.
    D. Alice is terrified Roger will find out about her recent drug use and sexual encounter with Bill.

7. Alice gets sleeping pills from her doctor, but admits she doesn't really need the sleep. What is it she says she needs instead?
    A. Alice needs a way to make extra money and she can do that buy selling her sleeping pills to kids at school.
    B. Alice needs an escape from her life and the sleeping pills allow her to have that.
    C. Alice needs a way to get Richie to like her and by giving him sleeping pills for free he seems more interested in dating her.
    D. Alice needs more energy and if she takes several pills at once, she has enough energy to stay alert all day.

8. Who is Chris?
    A. Chris is a girl Alice met at a local clothing boutique. The two hit it off and become friends.
    B. Chris is a boy at Alice's new school. She really likes him and is trying to get to know him better in hopes that they can date.
    C. Chris is a girl that babysits Alice's younger brother and sister. She acts sweet and the family really loves her, making Alice feel like she is losing her place in the family.
    D. Chris is a boy that supplies Alice with drugs. Alice gets pot and other drugs from him to turn around and sell at her school for a profit.

9. What is Alice's first job?
    A. Working at a clothing boutique
    B. Working the cash register at a small grocery store
    C. Working as a waitress at a local diner
    D. Working at an art gallery

Go Ask Alice Multiple Choice Questions for Assignment 2 page 3

10. How does Alice get through the long, stressful days of school and work while also dealing with her parents when she gets home?
    A. Alice has to combine drugs and alcohol to create the perfect high to get her through the whole day.
    B. Alice takes drugs at night to survive work and her parents and then uses the day at school to come off the high.
    C. Alice has to take drugs to keep her alert at school and in social situations and then tranquilizers to mellow out when she gets home.
    D. Alice has to skip classes at school to get some sleep and uses drugs to stay awake and friendly while at work and in front of her parents.

11. According to Alice's friend, why do more kids prefer drugs to alcohol?
    A. Drugs give people a much better high than alcohol.
    B. Drugs are easier for teenagers to get than alcohol.
    C. Alcohol can be much more addictive than drugs.
    D. Alcohol is more expensive than drugs.

12. Why does Alice decide not to go to college?
    A. Alice feels like her boyfriend, Richie, needs her help. She decides not to go to college so she can help him earn money to pay for his medical degree.
    B. Alice feels like school is too hard and not worth the effort. She likes the job she already has and figures she can work there for the rest of her life.
    C. Alice knows that if she goes to college her dad will know everything she does since he is a professor. She decides to skip college and have more privacy from her parents.
    D. Alice knows that college will cost a lot of money. If she uses the money she has saved, she can get a cool apartment and buy a lot of drugs.

13. Alice begins to sell drugs to help her boyfriend earn money. Who does she sell drugs to that makes her feel really guilty and upset?
    A. Her sister's friends
    B. Her little brother
    C. Elementary school students
    D. Homeless people

14. Describe the life Alice and Chris are living in San Francisco.
    A. Alice and Chris are always high. They have no money for rent and live on the streets.
    B. Alice and Chris have made several friends and are on their way to opening their own clothing boutique. They both couldn't be happier away from home.
    C. Alice and Chris fight all the time. The two hardly get along and are trying to find separate apartments.
    D. Alice and Chris live in a small, dirty apartment. They both work very hard all day long and are living life very differently than they expected.

Go Ask Alice Multiple Choice Questions for Assignment 3

Assignment #3
November 19-End of Diary One
1. After vowing to never do drugs again, Alice and Chris get mixed up in the drug scene in San Francisco. What event prompts the two friends to begin using drugs again?
    A. Alice and Chris meet two boys they think are cute. They go on a double date and discover the boys have a stash of pot. They want the older boys to think they are mature, so they smoke with them.
    B. Chris's boss, Shelia, invites the girls to a party. When the girls get to the party they realize people are passing around joints and can't resist.
    C. Alice and Chris are both depressed about their life in San Francisco. Chris is able to get pot from a friend and the girls vow to use it just once to give them a little pick up.
    D. Mr. Mellani's son comes into the store one day worried his father might discover his drug habit. He gives Alice some joints to hold so that he won't get caught. Alice and Chris can't resist and figure since it was free they should smoke it.

2. What happens to Alice and Chris that makes them leave San Francisco?
    A. The two girls are high all the time and loose their jobs for not going to work. Because of this, they have no money to pay rent and are evicted from their apartment. They leave to make a fresh start somewhere new.
    B. Alice gets a phone call from her parents. The girls are worried that since their parents know where they are that they will make them go home. They leave the city to hide from their parents once again.
    C. Richie and some friends show up and threaten to kill Alice if she doesn't start selling drugs for him once again. The girls are terrified and flee the city that night.
    D. The two girls are raped and sadistically brutalized by Shelia and her boyfriend while they are high one night. After being taken advantage of, they decide to leave.

3. Describe the new shop Alice and Chris open near Berkeley.
    A. They sell jewelry in a small shop near the college. They get a reputation in the town and begin to make even more money selling drugs to college kids.
    B. They open a shop that goes bankrupt soon after opening. They are forced to find new jobs to make money for the rent.
    C. They open a shop where college kids stop by to watch TV and sit around. There is a regular crowd and the business is fairly successful.
    D. They open a clothing shop that draws several wealthy women. The girls makes so much money they open a part for children as well.

Go Ask Alice Multiple Choice Questions for Assignment 3 page 2

4. What is Alice's life at home like when she returns from California?
    A. Alice's parents feel awkward around her. They don't want to push her, but they want to know what happened to her while she was away.
    B. Alice is welcomed home by her entire family. They all cry and are happy to see her. It is Christmas and Alice appreciates every moment with her family. They seem to get along with no problems and are just happy to be reunited.
    C. Alice's family cries and seem happy to see her, but after a few days at home continue nagging her and getting on her nerves. They try to get along for a short time, and then go back to fighting nonstop.
    D. Alice's family is happy to see her, but also worried she will leave again. They watch her like a hawk and don't allow her to go anywhere without them.

5. What is the best part of the New Year's Eve party Alice's parents throw?
    A. Several of the guests bring their kids. One of the boys has pot and offers some to Alice. A small group of kids escape the boring party and go outside to get high. This is the first time Alice has had drugs since coming home and enjoys every minute of it.
    B. Several of the guest bring their kids. One of the boys has pot and offers some to Alice. For the first time in her life, Alice is able to say no. She feels very proud of herself and optimistic that she will change her life.
    C. Before all the guests arrive, Alice and her family work together to get everything ready. She works in the kitchen with her mother and grandmother and enjoys feeling like a grown up woman. She imagines how it will be with her own family one day.
    D. After all the guests leave, Alice and her family put on the their pajamas and clean up the mess. The family laughs and goofs off, having fun together naturally. This is Alice's favorite part of the whole party.

6. How do other students react when Alice returns to school?
    A. Several kids harass Alice and try to get her to sell them drugs like she used to. They don't believe she is clean.
    B. Most of her friends are happy to see her. They go out of their way to provide extra support for her in keeping her away from people who use drugs.
    C. Alice is a grade level behind so none of her old friends will talk to her. The younger kids have all heard rumors about her drug use and don't want to talk to her either.
    D. Everyone ignores her. They are mad she left so suddenly and angry she never tried to call or contact them while gone.

7. Alice confides to her mom that kids at school are pressuring her to use drugs. What do her parents do to provide additional support?
    A. They plan fun activities, like going to the mountains, to keep her busy.
    B. They try to eat dinner together as a family each night to bring them closer together.
    C. They begin seeing a family therapist to help them become a stronger family.
    D. They talk to the parents of other teenagers to get them to stop pressuring Alice.

Go Ask Alice Multiple Choice Questions for Assignment 3 page 3

8. Why does Alice have to see a shrink?
    A. Knowing about her previous drug history, the school will only allow Alice to return if she sees a psychologist. The school requires a weekly update on her progress as part of the bargain to go back to school.
    B. Alice is having nightmares about her life on drugs. Her doctor recommends a psychologist to help her work through her fears and stop the nightmares.
    C. Chris's house gets raided by the police one night while Chris and Alice are high. Since it is her first offense, Alice's parents make a bargain with the court to send her to a psychologist instead of going to court.
    D. Alice is having a hard time adjusting to life at home. Her parents make her go to a psychologist so she can find ways to regain her old life.

9. What is Alice's situation at home like when she decides to run away again?
    A. Alice's parents are on the verge of a divorce. She blames herself for the stress and arguments and knows they will be happier with her gone.
    B. Alice's parents have her on probation. They watch everything she does and she can't talk to any of her friends or do anything without her parent's supervision.
    C. Alice and her parents are getting along better than ever. They trust her decisions and work to communicate with her on a regular basis.
    D. Alice's drug use has influenced her younger brother and sister. She finds out that they use drugs and can't handle the stress of knowing they were only following her lead.

10. After Alice runs away a second time, she continues writing but not in her diary. What does she use instead?
    A. Old newspapers from the park she sleeps in at night
    B. A new notebook she buys since she left her old diary at home
    C. A laptop she steals from an unsuspecting family on vacation
    D. Single sheets of paper, paper bags, and other items that happen to be around

11. What are the three places Alice lives when she runs away for a second time?
    A. Denver, Colorado; Coos Bay, Oregon; Southern California
    B. New York City, New York; Boston, Massachusetts; Philadelphia, Pennsylvania
    C. San Francisco, California; Los Angeles, California; Seattle, Washington
    D. Chicago, Illinois; Milwaukee, Wisconsin; St. Louis, Missouri

12. Where does Alice sleep when she runs away for a second time?
    A. In the dumpster behind a grocery store
    B. With a boy she meets and begins dating
    C. At a church that allows drug users as safe place to sleep
    D. At a place she shares with other drug users or in the park

Go Ask Alice Multiple Choice Questions for Assignment 3 page 4

13. What do the people at the mission do for Alice?
    A. Let her take a shower, give her clothes, feed her, take her to the doctor
    B. Give her a safe place to sleep and money for food
    C. Take her to the doctor and call her parents to come get her immediately
    D. Give her a job cleaning and cooking food for some extra money

14. How does Alice get money to buy drugs?
    A. She sells drugs for her dealer
    B. She works at a gas station four days a week
    C. She begs for money and performs sexual favors
    D. She steals from tourists

15. Alice is worried that with all the sex she is having she may get pregnant. Why can't she take the birth control pill to protect herself?
    A. Alice knows that she has to be 18 in order to get the pill. Since it is too hard to get illegally and she is not yet an adult, she can't take it.
    B. Alice uses so many drugs and blacks out so often that she can rarely tell what day it is. She can't take the pill for protection unless she can remember to take it each day, so she just hopes she doesn't end up pregnant.
    C. Alice tries taking the pill and realizes that it takes away from her high. She doesn't want to lose her great highs, so she won't take it.
    D. Alice's doctor warns her that the pill will react badly with the drugs she uses. She could die from the combination of the two drugs, so she can't take it.

16. Why does Alice want to get a new diary when she gets back home?
    A. Alice feels like her first diary is her past, or her life on drugs. When she gets home she wants to start a new diary that will be her future, a life without drugs.
    B. Alice's old diary is already full. She needs a new one in order to have enough room to write all her thoughts.
    C. Alice lost her old diary when she ran away so she needs a new one to have a place to write her thoughts.
    D. Alice's old diary is falling apart from being used so often. She needs to start a new one so she doesn't lose pages from her old one.

17. What career path does Alice decide to take when she graduates from high school?
    A. A pharmacist
    B. A social worker
    C. A doctor that works with the poor and homeless
    D. A guidance counselor or psychologist

Go Ask Alice Multiple Choice Questions for Assignment 4

Assignment #4
<u>Diary Number Two-July 3</u>

1. How does Alice perform as a student when she returns to school?
    A. She struggles to make up all the work she missed. She makes several low grades since she is so far behind.
    B. She continues as an average student making average grades just like she did before she left.
    C. She becomes a devoted student who studies several hours each night. She makes high grades in all her classes.
    D. She does really well in her elective classes, but still has a hard time with her grades in classes like math and English.

2. What special act does Alice do for her mother's birthday?
    A. Alice takes piano lessons without her mother knowing. She then surprises her mother with a song on her birthday.
    B. Alice cooks an entire meal all by herself as a surprise for her mother's birthday.
    C. Alice shows her mother her old diary to let her know all that she has been through. She does this to hopefully bring them closer together.
    D. Alice takes her mother horseback riding for the first time. Her mother had wanted to go horseback riding since she was a child, but had never been.

3. How can the reader tell the kids at school don't believe that Alice is really through with drugs?
    A. The kids who are on drugs ask her to parties while the kids who are not on drugs won't talk to her since they still consider her a druggie.
    B. Several of her old friends keep giving her free drugs, knowing she won't be able to resist.
    C. The kids who are not on drugs refuse to work on any assignments or projects with Alice because they are afraid she might try to give them drugs without their knowledge.
    D. The kids who are on drugs are afraid to be near Alice since they don't want to get caught with their own drugs and the kids who are not on drugs are afraid to be near Alice because they think she will trick them into doing drugs.

4. What type of file does Alice start that will help her with her goal of becoming a counselor?
    A. A file of ways for adults to communicate with teenagers
    B. A file of all the different types of drugs and their effect on teenagers
    C. A file of personal stories about people who have used drugs
    D. A file of statistics relating to kids and drug use

Go Ask Alice Multiple Choice Questions for Assignment 4 page 2

5. When Alice's grandpa dies, she has morbid thoughts and nightmares about him. What does she dwell on about death in these thoughts and nightmares?
    A. The decay of the body with worms and maggots feeding on the flesh
    B. The idea of being buried alive and clawing at the casket to get out
    C. The idea of being in a casket with no air and suffocating
    D. The possibility of coming back from the dead to haunt old enemies

6. How does Alice meet Joel?
    A. Alice begins taking piano lessons once again. Her teacher was sick one day and referred her to Joel for a substitute lesson.
    B. Alice volunteers in her sister's elementary school as part of her agreement with the court. She meets Joel also volunteering at the school.
    C. Alice and her mother are out picking up a prescription for her grandmother. She meets Joel when he helps them in the pharmacy.
    D. Alice's dad gets special permission for her to use the university library. While she is there studying one afternoon she meets Joel.

7. How does Joel fit in with Alice and her family?
    A. No one in her family likes him because he is so much older than Alice. They don't like it when he comes over to the house and trys to make up reasons why he can't see Alice.
    B. Joel feels comfortable having dinners with the family and long discussions with her father. He seems to get along well with everyone in the family and shows Alice a lot of respect.
    C. Joel gets along great with her father, but her mother is worried they are moving to fast. She feels like Joel is pressuring Alice for more in the relationship and using her to get a scholarship from her dad.
    D. Alice's parents like him but her younger brother and sister think he is rude. They feel like he ignores them and is a bad match for Alice.

8. What happened while Alice was babysitting for Mrs. Larsen?
    A. Someone tries to break into the house. Alice grabs the baby and locks herself in the bathroom until Mrs. Larsen gets home later that night.
    B. Jan comes by stoned and wanting to take over the babysitting job. Alice is worried about the safety of the baby so she calls Jan's mom to come get her and take her home.
    C. The baby starts to choke as Alice is feeding him. She calls 911, but in the meantime gives him CPR to save his life.
    D. Jan comes by with some pot. Since the baby is already asleep, Jan convinces Alice to break down and try drugs for the first time since she has been back home.

Go Ask Alice Multiple Choice Questions for Assignment 4 page 3

9. What do the kids at school threaten to do to Alice's family?
    A. They threaten to severely beat up her siblings and burn down her family's home.
    B. They threaten to start dangerous rumors about her family to force them out of town.
    C. They threaten to give her younger siblings candy laced with drugs and plant drugs in her father's car so he will get fired.
    D. They threaten to hurt her fragile grandmother since she lives alone.

10. What do the kids at school do to Alice to try and get her in trouble with the principal?
    A. They fake a fight and make it look like Alice attacked another student.
    B. Someone replaces Alice's research paper with a fake, making it look like she copied it straight from the encyclopedia.
    C. Someone places a burning roach in her locker, trying to make it look like she had drugs with her at school so she would get in trouble.
    D. They spray paint profanity on the walls of the school then hide the empty can of paint in Alice's locker to frame her.

11. What happens to Alice as she is taking a walk in the park?
    A. She runs into her exboyfriend and drug dealer, Rickie. He punches her several times as payback for stealing money from him.
    B. A guy Alice doesn't even know grabs her by the arm and threatens her for being a fink. He then takes her behind the bushes and kisses her, threatening to do more.
    C. She has a flashback of her past and passes out. Someone finds her and calls for help. She is rushed to the hospital and gets three stitches from the fall.
    D. Roger runs up behind her and gives her a hug. He came home from military school for the summer and had been looking for Alice all over town.

12. What do Joel and Alice exchange as symbols of their relationship before he leaves to go home for the summer?
    A. Joel gives Alice a promise ring and Alice gives Joel a poem she wrote for him.
    B. Joel gives Alice a kitten and Alice gives Joel a the key to the lockbox that contains her old diary.
    C. Joel shows Alice a tattoo he got of a heart with her initials and Alice promises to get the same the next day.
    D. Joel gives Alice a gold watch his father had given him and Alice gives Joel a ring that belonged to her grandmother.

13. What happened to Chris?
    A. Chris's parents moved her to a town where no one knew about her past.
    B. Chris graduated from high school and moved to New York for college.
    C. Chris ran away from home again and no one knows where she went.
    D. Chris died from a drug overdose shortly after she and Alice return home.

Go Ask Alice Multiple Choice Questions for Assignment 5

Assignment #5
July 7- Epilogue
1. Why does Mrs. Larsen need Alice to babysit, cook, and clean for her?
    A. Mrs. Larsen is pregnant again and needs someone to help her out so she can get more rest.
    B. Mrs. Larsen broke her leg in a car accident and needs someone to take care of the house while she heals.
    C. Mrs. Larsen decided to go back to work and needed help around the house while she was at work.
    D. Mrs. Larsen has to go out of town to take care of her sick mother. She needs someone to help out until she returns home.

2. Describe the physical condition Alice is in at the hospital.
    A. Alice has third degree burns covering her arms and hands, her jaw is broken and wired shut so she can hardly speak, her ankle is broken, and she has blurry vision.
    B. Alice has a broken nose, her eyelids are bruised and swollen so that she can barely even see, she is missing a lot of hair, both her feet are broken, and she has to have four teeth replaced.
    C. Alice has two broken ribs, her leg is broken in two places, she has bruises all over her body, there are stitches covering most of her face, and she has a mild case of amnesia.
    D. Alice has torn off the tops of her fingers, she is missing fingernails, her face is scratched and clawed up, she is missing chunks of her hair and her scalp is exposed, her body is badly bruised, and several of her toes are broken.

3. How did Alice end up on the bad acid trip that landed her in the hospital?
    A. She ate some chocolate covered peanuts that were on the counter at the Larsen house. She thought they were a gift from Mr. Larsen and didn't know someone had covered them in acid.
    B. Chris comes back into town for a visit and goes to visit Alice. Chris gives Alice some pills to take and swears they aren't addictive. Alice takes them and discovers that they have been laced with something bad.
    C. Alice brushes her teeth in the morning before going to babysit. Little did she know Marcie and some friends had snuck into the house and placed acid on her toothbrush to get back at her from snitching.
    D. Alice finds acid in the Larsen house when she is looking for the remote control. She can't resist the urge and takes some of the acid, not knowing it was bad.

Go Ask Alice Multiple Choice Questions for Assignment 5 page 2

4. Describe the hallucination Alice had while on a bad acid trip and how the hallucination correlates with her injuries.
    A. Alice imagines she is on fire. She runs around the house beating her body against walls to put the fire out, causing the broken bones and bruising.
    B. Alice imagines being covered in worms and maggots. She tries to get them off of her but is really pulling off pieces of her skin and hair.
    C. Alice imagines being in a hockey game. She throws herself at furniture and doors, knocking out some teeth and bruising herself badly.
    D. Alice imagines she is being chased by bears. She runs madly through the house falling down stairs and running into walls, causing broken bones and damage to her whole body.

5. Alice claims she did not take the drugs on purpose and was tricked. Knowing her history of drugs and running away, what do Alice's parents think?
    A. Alice's parents don't believe her at first but then change their mind.
    B. Alice parents don't believe her.
    C. Alice's parents believe her after they talk to Marcie and Jan.
    D. Alice's parents believe her immediately.

6. Alice's case is heard before the court to determine what will happen to her when she is released from the hospital. Aside from the previous drug charge on her record, what other evidence is presented to the judge to make him rule against Alice?
    A. Marcie and Jan both take the stand. They lie to the judge and tell him Alice has been trying to sell them drugs for weeks.
    B. The police search Alice's room and find drugs hidden in a book on her shelf. Someone planted them there, but no one knows who.
    C. The judge demands that Alice's diary be read before the court. After hearing her earlier entries about her intensive drug use, he assumes that this encounter was not an accident.
    D. While Alice is still on her bad trip she confesses to using drugs. The nurses record her statement and give it to the judge at the hearing.

7. When Alice finds out she is going to be placed in the state mental hospital, how does she feel?
    A. She is nervous about going to a new place and meeting new people, but she knows she needs to get help before she can live a normal life.
    B. She is terrified to be placed in a mental hospital. She doesn't think she is crazy and feels she doesn't belong there.
    C. She is excited to get out of the regular hospital. She hates the nurses and can't stand being alone in her room. She feels the mental hospital has to be better.
    D. She is happy to be going to the mental hospital. She knows there will be other recovering drug users and figures someone will smuggle in pot.

Go Ask Alice Multiple Choice Questions for Assignment 5 page 3

8. The youth section of the mental hospital classifies patients into Group One and Group Two. What is the difference between these two groups?
    A. The groups are determined by how long a patient has been there. The Group One patients have been there more than a year, Group Two patients less than a year.
    B. The groups are determined by why patients are in the hospital. The Group One patients are all drug users. Group Two patients are victims of real mental illnesses.
    C. The groups are determined by behavior. The Group One patients have proved they can behave and get special privileges, while the Group Two patients are on probation.
    D. The groups are determined by sex. The girls are all placed in Group One while the boys are in a separate area in Group Two.

9. Why does Alice begin interviewing the other patients at the hospital?
    A. She has been given a position on the newspaper at the school within the hospital. She is writing feature stories so patients can get to know each other better.
    B. She is bored in the hospital and desperate to make new friends. She begins interviewing people to get to know them and build friendships.
    C. Her parents tell her to start talking to other patients to prove she is interacting and getting better, that way the judge will let her out sooner.
    D. Her doctor tells her that if she really wants to be a social worker she should start interviewing other patients to help her better understand others.

10. Alice becomes friends with a young girl named Babbie while staying at the hospital. What surprising news does Alice discover about Babbie's parents?
    A. Babbie's parents don't want her to live with them anymore. They are putting her into a foster home instead.
    B. Babbie's parents blame each other for her drug use. They are divorced and both think the other wasn't watching her close enough.
    C. Babbie's parents are getting divorced because of her drug habit. They have fought over her problem too much and have ruined their relationship in the process.
    D. Babbie's parents are suing the hospital. She was in the mental hospital once before and they are angry she was released without being treated properly. She began using drugs even more than before she was hospitalized.

11. Who writes Alice a ten page letter while she is in the hospital? What does the letter say?
    A. Chris writes Alice a letter telling her about a rehabilitation program she went through and how it has changed her life.
    B. Alice's brother writes Alice a letter telling her how he is being pressured to take drugs at his middle school.
    C. Marcie writes Alice a letter apologizing for putting acid on the peanuts and then lying to the judge to get her sent to a mental hospital.
    D. Joel writes Alice a letter telling her that he forgives her and understands about her past.

Go Ask Alice Multiple Choice Questions for Assignment 5 page 4

12. When Alice gets back home she begins to pray. Aside from herself, who does she ask God to help?
    A. Her mom and dad
    B. Her brother and sister
    C. Jan and Marcie
    D. Babbie and the others still at the mental hospital

13. Why do Alice and her family take a trip to the east coast for a couple weeks?
    A. Alice's dad gets the chance to cover a class for another professor for a few weeks. The family goes along to make it a vacation.
    B. Alice feels weird being back at home. Her parents take the family on a trip to get her mind off of the mental hospital and allow her to adjust to life with her family.
    C. Alice's cousin is getting married. The family uses the wedding to get out of town and see more of the country, trying to rebuild a family bond.
    D. Alice is desperate to see Joel. Her family takes a trip to the east coast for a vacation that will allow her to stop and spend a few days with Joel.

14. Who is Fawn?
    A. Fawn is Joel's old girlfriend. Alice finds out that when Joel went back home he got back together with his high school sweetheart.
    B. Fawn is one of the "straight kids" from school. She asks Alice to hang out and the two become close friends.
    C. Fawn is the new therapist Alice is seeing. She is still required to go to therapy even though she was released from the mental hospital.
    D. Fawn is one of the kitten's that belongs to Alice's sister. She seems to like Alice and follows her everywhere.

15. Why does Alice's piano teacher call?
    A. Alice still owes the piano teacher money from the lessons she took before she was hospitalized. Her teacher is trying to find out when Alice will be able to pay her.
    B. The piano teacher wants Alice to play a solo in an upcoming concert. She also wants to use Alice's photo on the cover of the program.
    C. The piano teacher is overwhelmed with students. She knows Alice is a good piano player and asks her if she wants to earn extra money by helping teach some of the beginner classes.
    D. Alice used to babysit the piano teacher's daughter. The piano teacher is calling to see if Alice can babysit later that week.

16. What does Alice's family do for her birthday?
    A. Alice's parents buy her all new clothes for the upcoming school year.
    B. Alice's parents give her a car for her birthday.
    C. Alice's parents throw her a party and surprise her by having Joel come.
    D. Alice's parents take her to the beach for her birthday.

Go Ask Alice Multiple Choice Questions for Assignment 5 page 5

17. What happens after Alice decides not to keep a diary?
    A. Nine months after Alice stops keeping a diary her and Joel have a baby and decide to get married.
    B. Five months after Alice stops keeping a diary she is back into drugs. She later finds out she has contracted AIDS from sharing needles with other users.
    C. Six weeks after Alice stops keeping a diary she runs away from home and is never heard from again.
    D. Three weeks after Alice stops keeping a diary she is found dead from an overdose on drugs.

ANSWER KEY - MULTIPLE CHOICE STUDY/QUIZ QUESTIONS
Go Ask Alice

	Assignment 1	Assignment 2	Assignment 3	Assignment 4	Assignment 5
1	B	B	B	C	B
2	D	D	D	B	D
3	C	B	C	A	A
4	D	A	B	D	B
5	A	C	D	A	D
6	B	D	A	D	A
7	C	B	A	B	B
8	A	A	C	B	C
9	B	A	B	C	D
10	D	C	D	C	A
11	B	B	A	B	D
12	A	A	D	D	C
13	A	C	A	A	A
14	C	D	C	X	B
15	X	X	B	X	B
16	X	X	A	X	C
17	X	X	D	X	D

PREREADING VOCABULARY WORKSHEETS

VOCABULARY Sept 16-July 10 *Go Ask Alice*

Part I: Using Prior Knowledge and Contextual Clues

Below are the sentences in which the vocabulary words appear in the text. Read the sentence. Use any clues you can find in the sentence combined with your prior knowledge, and write what you think the underlined words mean on the lines provided.

1. Even my parents treat me like I'm stupid and <u>inferior</u> and ever short.
_____

2. Everything's dull. Maybe it's just because I'm growing up and life is becoming more <u>blase</u>.
_____

3. Not one bite of chocolate or <u>nary</u> a french fried potato will pass my lips till I've lost ten globby pounds of lumpy lard.
_____

4. I've seen pictures of it, but it still seems like a large, cold, <u>foreboding</u> stranger.
_____

5. How can I possibly be such a dud when I come from this <u>gregarious</u>, friendly, elastic background?
_____

6. She's as <u>cloddy</u> and misfitting as I am.
_____

7. I could see them all squirming a little even as I have been squirming ever since we got to this <u>impregnable</u> hole.
_____

8. Beth is really <u>conscientious</u> and worries about her grades so we did some work and then listened to records and drank no-calorie cokes.
_____

9. Mother took me shopping and let me spend five dollars on a little solid gold necklace with a personal <u>inscription</u> engraved inside.
_____

10. . . . I'd never really belonged in her crowd which were kind of the top <u>echelon</u>, ...
_____

Go Ask Alice Vocabulary Worksheet Sept 16-July 10 Continued

Part II: Determining the Meaning
    Match the vocabulary words to their dictionary definitions

___ 1. inferior	A. strong feeling of coming misfortune or evil
___ 2. blase	B. stupid or of lesser dignity or value
___ 3. nary	C. bored with life or unimpressed
___ 4. foreboding	D. unable to be captured, overthrown, or broken into
___ 5. gregarious	E. marking of words or message on an item
___ 6. cloddy	F. lower in position, rank, or worth
___ 7. impregnable	G. level of command, authority, or rank
___ 8. conscientious	H. characterized by taking extreme care and/or making great effort
___ 9. inscription	I. not any; no; never
___ 10. echelon	J. seeking the company of others; outgoing and sociable

VOCABULARY July 13-November 16 *Go Ask Alice*

Part I: Using Prior Knowledge and Contextual Clues

Below are the sentences in which the vocabulary words appear in the text. Read the sentence. Use any clues you can find in the sentence combined with your prior knowledge, and write what you think the underlined words mean on the lines provided.

1. It's a completely new world I'm exploring, and you can't even <u>conceive</u> the wide new doors that are opening up before me.
   _____

2. I just sat in the corner feeling left out and sort of <u>antagonistic</u>, then suddenly it happened and I wanted to dance . . ..
   _____

3. & 4. If I were only a Catholic maybe I could do some kind of terrible <u>penance</u> to pay for my <u>transgressions</u>.
   _____
   _____

5. & 6. It was a sound unsimilar to any I have ever heard, and I remember trying desperately to give a <u>dissertation</u> upon the <u>phenomena</u> of each individual hair having perfect pitch within itself.
   _____
   _____

7. . . . without having some idiot <u>fink</u> find out where or what our bag is.
   _____

8. I'm not being <u>vindictive</u> or spiteful or jealous, really I'm not.
   _____

9. We are in San Francisco, in a dirty smelling and <u>stifling</u> little one room apartment.
   _____

10. . . . I'm with Chris and they think she's a nice and respectable girl who won't lead me <u>astray</u>.
    _____

Go Ask Alice Vocabulary Worksheet July 13-November 16 Continued

Part II: Determining the Meaning
    Match the vocabulary words to their dictionary definitions

___ 1. conceive	A.	lengthy, formal speech or writing about a particular topic
___ 2. antagonistic	B.	revengeful, with the desire to hurt another
___ 3. penance	C.	imagine; form an idea of
___ 4. transgressions	D.	violation of a laws or duties
___ 5. dissertation	E.	off or away from the correct or right path
___ 6. phenomena	F.	informer, spy, or someone who squeals
___ 7. fink	G.	act of devotion to pay for a sin or wrongdoing
___ 8. vindictive	H.	something that is remarkable, impressive, or extraordinary
___ 9. stifling	I.	smothering or suffocating
___ 10. astray	J.	hostile, unfriendly

VOCABULARY November 19-End of Diary One *Go Ask Alice*

Part I: Using Prior Knowledge and Contextual Clues
 Below are the sentences in which the vocabulary words appear in the text. Read the sentence. Use any clues you can find in the sentence combined with your prior knowledge, and write what you think the underlined words mean on the lines provided.

1. I felt gentle and drowsy and wonderfully soft like I was floating above reality and the mundane things were lost forever in space.
_____

2. I feel like the prodigal son being welcomed back into the fold, and I shall never ever go away again.
_____

3. They have accepted me as an individual, as a personality, as an entity. I belong!
_____

4. It [being a teenager] is a difficult, lost, vacillating time.
_____

5. . . . I surely would not have either the strength or the fortitude to get through that number again.
_____

6. Doris and I are both going to cut out of this asinine assed place.
_____

7. And there were no recriminations or scoldings or lectures or anything.
_____

8. Sometimes I think that [hairstyle] was our biggest bone of contention.
_____

9. Someone evil and foul and degenerate wrote in my book, took over my life.
_____

10. I have lamented until I am dehydrated . . ..
_____

Go Ask Alice Vocabulary Worksheet November 19-End of Diary One Continued

Part II: Determining the Meaning
   Match the vocabulary words to their dictionary definitions

___ 1. mundane   A. accusations in response to accusation from someone else
___ 2. prodigal   B. something that exists as its own self or being
___ 3. entity   C. mental and emotional strength in facing difficulty
___ 4. vacillating   D. one who falls below the desirable level of quality
___ 5. fortitude   E. disagreement; point of disagreement
___ 6. asinine   F. indecisive; unsteady; wavering
___ 7. recriminations   G. express grief or regret; mourn
___ 8. contention   H. foolish; silly; stupid
___ 9. degenerate   I. common, boring, dull, unimaginative
___ 10. lamented   J. wastefully extravagant

VOCABULARY Diary Number Two-July 3 *Go Ask Alice*

Part I: Using Prior Knowledge and Contextual Clues
   Below are the sentences in which the vocabulary words appear in the text. Read the sentence. Use any clues you can find in the sentence combined with your prior knowledge, and write what you think the underlined words mean on the lines provided.

1. It was a revelation! Without drugs!
_____

2. I was a shooting star, a comet piercing the firmament, blazing through the sky.
_____

3. None of the kids think I'm going to stay off, because most of those who've been busted before are just being more careful and discreet.
_____

4. Worms don't make distinction under the ground.
_____

5. I told him that women were very perceptive, that's all.
_____

6. Dad had absolutely the most wonderful news to tell at dinner! (And he did it very nonchalantly.)
_____

7. Oh, I am sick, I'm sick of the screwed up potheads and acidheads and all the other dopey dopers who are persecuting me.
_____

8. Jan sidled up to me as I was walking down the ramp and whispered . . . .
_____

9. Even George, who used to take me out, now looks at me with disdain or passes me by without even seeing me.
_____

10. I feel like we're under siege and no one else seems to be taking it very seriously.
_____

Go Ask Alice Vocabulary Worksheet Diary Number Two-July 3 Continued

Part II: Determining the Meaning
   Match the vocabulary words to their dictionary definitions

   ___ 1. revelation   A. understanding with insight or intuition
   ___ 2. firmament   B. pursuing with harassment; annoying persistently
   ___ 3. discreet   C. showing wise self- restraint in behavior
   ___ 4. distinction   D. the feeling that someone or something is unworthy of one's
                                consideration or respect
   ___ 5. perceptive   E. something that is uncovered, not previously known
   ___ 6. nonchalantly   F. recognizing or distinguishing differences
   ___ 7. persecuting   G. edged or moved up sideways
   ___ 8. sidled   H. the expanse of the sky
   ___ 9. disdain   I. in a way cooly unconcerned, indifferent, or casual
   ___ 10. siege   J. assault; attack

VOCABULARY July 7- Epilogue *Go Ask Alice*

Part I: Using Prior Knowledge and Contextual Clues

Below are the sentences in which the vocabulary words appear in the text. Read the sentence. Use any clues you can find in the sentence combined with your prior knowledge, and write what you think the underlined words mean on the lines provided.

1. His two eye sockets were teeming with white soft-bodied, creeping animals.
   _____

2. The night was interminable. Anything in the world could happen in here and no one would ever know.
   _____

3. This morning they woke me up at 6:30 for a breakfast I couldn't eat and bleary eyed and still shivering, I was led down the long dark hall to the big metal door with the barred window in the middle.
   _____

4. One older woman in the ward is a lecherous alcoholic and she frightens me but I'm worried even more for Babbie.
   _____

5. They are like the ravings of the idiotic spewing woman who is now part of my intimate family.
   _____

6. . . . she tried to monopolize people and was always clinging to them and hanging onto them.
   _____

7. I'm still not sure I want to go prying into other people's lives.
   _____

8. Tom is a handsome, likeable, extremely articulate young guy.
   _____

9. Dad also said that he finally got Jan to sign an affidavit saying that I wasn't pushing at the school.
   _____

10. Mom was right. My premonitions about Fawn's party were completely ridiculous.
    _____

Go Ask Alice Vocabulary Worksheet July 7- Epilogue Continued

Part II: Determining the Meaning
Match the vocabulary words to their dictionary definitions

___ 1. teeming
___ 2. interminable
___ 3. bleary
___ 4. lecherous
___ 5. ravings
___ 6. monopolize
___ 7. prying
___ 8. articulate
___ 9. affidavit
___ 10. premonitions

A. to have complete possession of; to dominate
B. a written statement or declaration made under oath
C. full of things; swarming
D. wild, delirious, or frenzied talking
E. distinct, fluent, meaningful, and clear in the power of speech
F. suggestive; lustful
G. advance warnings of the future
H. unending
I. blurred from sleep or fatigue; unclear
J. looking at closely or curiously

VOCABULARY ANSWER KEY *Go Ask Alice*

	Vocabulary 1	Vocabulary 2	Vocabulary 3	Vocabulary 4	Vocabulary 5
1	F	C	I	E	C
2	C	J	J	H	H
3	I	G	B	C	I
4	A	D	F	F	F
5	J	A	C	A	D
6	B	H	H	I	A
7	D	F	A	B	J
8	H	B	E	G	E
9	E	I	D	D	B
10	G	E	G	J	G

DAILY LESSONS

LESSON ONE

Objectives
1. To introduce the *Go Ask Alice* unit
2. To distribute books, study questions, and other related materials
3. To preview the vocabulary and study questions for Assignment 1
4. To begin Assignment 1

Note: Lesson six calls for a guest speaker. Preview lesson six and make necessary arrangements.

Activity #1

Show students a 10-15 minute clip, or several shorter clips, from the Disney version of *Alice in Wonderland.* Ask students to talk about the rumors they have heard about the movie/book. Most will know the psychedelic colors and ideas are often associated with drugs. Prompt a discussion about what in the movie could be evidence of drug use, or appeal to those on drugs.

Activity #2

Next, place a copy of the lyrics to "White Rabbit," a popular song from the 60's by Jefferson Airplane, on the overhead projector. If possible, download the song from a valid internet source and have students listen to it as they follow along with the lyrics. Once the song is complete, talk about the meaning of the song, making sure to point out the repetitive line "Go Ask Alice."

Transition: Once you have discussed the movie *Alice in Wonderland* and the song "White Rabbit" tell your students they will be reading a book called *Go Ask Alice.* Tell students this book is the diary of an anonymous girl and her battle with drug use. Explain that the title came from the Jefferson Airplane song they just heard. Take a few minutes to talk about why the editor of this novel would choose to use the name Alice based on the two references just used in class.

Activity #3

Flip through the novel to show students that the book is written in diary format. Show students how each section begins with the date, followed by an entry about Alice's life that day. Tell students that Alice's journal entries are thoughtful reflections of her life that day, not just descriptions of what happened. Explain to students that they will be keeping a journal like Alice does, reflecting on how daily events and interactions shape their lives. Next, distribute the project requirements and discuss in detail.

Activity #4

Distribute the materials students will use in this unit. Explain in detail how students are to use these materials.

MATERIALS TO DISCUSS WITH STUDENTS

Study Guides Students should read the study guide questions for each reading assignment prior to beginning the reading assignment to get a feeling for what events and ideas are important in the section they are about to read. After reading the section, students will (as a class or individually) answer the questions to review the important events and ideas from that section of the book. Students should keep the study guides as study materials for the unit test. **Review the study questions for Assignment 1 while you're looking at the study guides.**

Vocabulary Prior to reading a reading assignment, students will do vocabulary work related to the section of the book they are about to read. Following the completion of the reading of the book, there will be a vocabulary review of all the words used in the vocabulary assignments. Students should keep their vocabulary work as study materials for the unit test. **Do Assignment 1 together orally to show students how to do the vocabulary worksheets.**

Reading Assignment Sheet You need to fill in the reading assignment sheet to let students know by when their reading has to be completed. You can either write the assignment sheet up on a side blackboard or bulletin board and leave it there for students to see each day, or you can make copies for each student to have. In either case, you should advise students to become very familiar with the reading assignments so they know what is expected of them.

Extra Activities Center The Unit Resource Materials portion of this LitPlan contains suggestions for an extra library of related books and articles in your classroom as well as crossword and word search puzzles. Make an extra activities center in your room where you will keep these materials for students to use. (Bring the books and articles in from the library and keep several copies of the puzzles on hand.) Explain to students that these materials are available for students to use when they finish reading assignments or other class work early.

Nonfiction Assignment Sheet Explain to students that they each are to read at least one non-fiction piece from the in-class library at some time during the unit. Students will fill out a nonfiction assignment sheet after completing the reading to help you (the teacher) evaluate their reading experiences and to help the students think about and evaluate their own reading experiences.

Books Each school has its own rules and regulations regarding student use of school books. Advise students of the procedures that are normal for your school. Preview the book. Look at the covers, front-matter, and index.
Activity #5
    Tell students that they should read Assignment 1 prior to the next class period. Give them the remainder of this class (if time remains) to complete this assignment.

Reflective Diary

Project Background
Go Ask Alice tells the story of Alice's life through a series of diary entries. Each diary entry varies in length, but usually contains some insight into Alice's life. Alice doesn't use her diary to simply record daily events; instead, she uses it to reflect on her life and growth from teenager to adult. Alice talks a lot about her actions and how they affect her life, her dreams, her communication with adults and family members, and her inner struggles and desires.

Project Assignment
You will be keeping a diary recording reflections about your life. Be sure to avoid just listing the events of your day, and focus on your thoughts and feelings about what's going on in your life.

Project Requirements

Cover
Take a sheet of construction paper to use as your cover. Write your name in the center of the paper. Next, cut words, phrases, and pictures out of magazines and newspapers that represent you and your personality. Arrange these cutouts in a collage fashion around your name. The cover should be a creative expression of your personality.

Entries
You will have a total of 20 diary entries. Each diary entry should be at least one full page. You may type the journal entries or write them by hand. Remember to not only recount the events of your day, but also how you felt about what happened. Analyze how the events of the day impacted your life. Talk about your feelings and thoughts as well as the events that took place during the day. Try to reflect on your relationship with your family and friends as Alice frequently does. Analyze how those relationships shape your life as well. Your diary entries should include content that is appropriate for school.

Organization
Once you have finished all 20 of your journal entries, place them in chronological order. Be sure your writing is neat and readable. Staple the cover you created to the front of your diary entries.

LESSON TWO

Objectives
1. To review main ideas, events, and vocabulary of Assignment 1
2. To bridge a connection between the novel and student's lives
3. To create a visual display that will be used during and after reading strategy
4. To preview the vocabulary and study questions for Assignment 2

Activity #1
Give students a few minutes to formulate answers for the study guide questions for Assignment 1, and then discuss the answers to the questions in detail. Write the answers on the board or overhead transparency so students can have the correct answers for study purposes.

NOTE: It is a good practice in public speaking and leadership skills for individual students to take charge of leading the discussions of the study questions. Perhaps a different student could go to the front of the class and lead the discussion each day that the study questions are discussed in this unit. Of course, you should guide the discussion when appropriate and try to fill in any gaps students may leave. The study questions could really be handled in a number of different ways, including in small groups with group reports following. Occasionally you may want to use the multiple choice questions as quizzes to check students' reading comprehension. As a short review now and then, students could pair up for the first (or last, if you have time left at the end of a class period) few minutes of class to quiz each other from the study questions. Mix up the methods of reviewing the materials and checking comprehension throughout the unit so students don't get bored just answering the questions the same way each day. Variety in methods will also help address the different learning styles of your students. From now on in this unit, the directions will simply say, "Discuss the answers to the study questions in detail as previously directed." You will choose the method of preparation and discussion each day based on what best suits you and your class.

Activity #2
Review the vocabulary answers from the reading. Make sure students write down the correct answers.

Activity #3
Give students construction paper and markers. Tell them they will be creating a time line for their life, but instead of using a straight line, they will use a line that goes up and down to various degrees to illustrate the high and low points of their life. The line should be continuous, but make steep climbs up for positive events, and drops down low for negative events, with mediocre events in the center (the line resembles the reading of an EKG). Tell students to place at least ten events on their time line and use the markers to provide an illustration for each event. After students have had sufficient time to complete this assignment, allow students the opportunity to share their time line with the class. Note: You may want to display these time lines in the classroom.

Activity #4
Once students have become familiar with creating a time line for their life, tell them they will be using this same method to create a class time line for Alice's life. Take a large piece of paper and cover a wall of the room. As a class, brainstorm events from the first portion of the reading that are significant enough to include on the time line. Determine how "high" or "low" to draw the line based on whether it was a positive or negative event. Allow different students to add different events, using illustrations when possible. Add to the class time line in this same manner after each reading assignment.

Activity #5
Review the study questions and vocabulary for Assignment 2 orally together in class. Tell students that they should read Assignment 2 prior to the next class period. Give them the remainder of this class (if time remains) to complete this assignment.

LESSON THREE

<u>Objectives</u>
1. To allow to students to express personal opinions using a topic discussed in *Go Ask Alice*
2. To enhance students' overall writing ability

<u>Activity #1</u>

In *Go Ask Alice*, Alice talks a lot about the influence friends have on the actions of her life. When she is trying to stay away from drugs, she works to hang out with the "straight" kids. When she is introduced to drugs and when she continues to fall deep into heavy drug use, she is surrounded by friends and boyfriends whose lives revolve around drugs. In this assignment, students will express their opinion on the influence of peers in their own lives. Distribute Writing Assignment #1 and use the Writing Evaluation Form included in this unit to give feedback to your students.

WRITING ASSIGNMENT #1 - *Go Ask Alice*
Writing to Express Personal Opinions

PROMPT
Alice talks a lot about the influence friends have on the actions of her life. When she is trying to stay away from drugs, she works to hang out with the "straight" kids. When she is introduced to drugs and when she continues to fall deep into heavy drug use, she is surrounded by friends and boyfriends whose lives revolve around drugs. Your assignment is to discuss the degree in which friends/peers influence your decisions.

PREWRITING
Think about the type of people you hang out with. Make a list of all the positive and negative things your friends have introduced to you or convinced you to do. Items on your list can be something simple like teaching you to eat sushi, or more complex like introducing you to a negative habit. Then, think about how your actions and choices are influenced by the people you hang out with. Determine how much you let your friends influence what you think and do.

DRAFTING
This essay should be written in first person. It will have an introductory paragraph where you will want to briefly mention the degree in which your friends influence your life.

The body of your essay should include several paragraphs providing support for your opinion. You will want to give multiple examples of ways your friends have, or haven't, influenced your actions and decisions. For each new example, begin a new paragraph.

Your essay should have a conclusion that contains a final summary on how much friends and peers influence your life. Try to leave a lasting impression with your reader with a powerful example or final point.

PROMPT
When you finish the rough draft of your composition, ask a student who sits near you to read it. After reading your rough draft, he/she should tell you what he/she liked best about your work, which parts were difficult to understand, and ways in which your work could be improved. Reread your paper considering your critic's comments, and make the corrections you think are necessary. Ask your classmate what he/she thought of each of the characters/events you chose for your assignment.

PROOFREADING
Do a final proofreading of your paper double-checking your grammar, spelling, organization, and the clarity of your ideas.

WRITING EVALUATION FORM - *Go Ask Alice*

Name _____ Date _____

Writing Assignment # _____   Grade _____

Circle One For Each Item:

Introduction:	excellent	good	fair	poor
Body Paragraphs:	excellent	good	fair	poor
Conclusion:	excellent	good	fair	poor
Grammar:	excellent	good	fair	poor
Spelling:	excellent	good	fair	poor
Punctuation:	excellent	good	fair	poor
Legibility:	excellent	good	fair	poor
_____	excellent	good	fair	poor
_____	excellent	good	fair	poor

Strengths:

Weaknesses:

Comments/Suggestions:

LESSON FOUR

<u>Objectives</u>
1. To review main ideas, events, and vocabulary of Assignment 2
2. To continue working on the time line
3. To have students research and read non-fiction related to the book to help connect the book to real life
4. To broaden students' knowledge about topics related to the book

<u>Activity #1</u>
Have students answer the study guide questions for reading Assignment 2 as previously directed.

<u>Activity #2</u>
Review the vocabulary answers from the reading. Make sure students write down the correct answers.

<u>Activity #3</u>
Add events from the reading to the time line as previously described.

<u>Activity #4</u>
Take students to the library or media center. With students, brainstorm a list of non-fiction topics that could be related to *Go Ask Alice*. A short list to get you started is included below.
- Drug addiction
- Peer pressure
- Real stories of teens who have overcome a drug addiction
- Real stories of teens who have succumbed to a drug addiction
- Statistics on teenage drug use
- How teenagers can get help
- Communication between teenagers and parents
- Information on teenagers who runaway from home
- Organizations that offer help/assistance to teenagers on drugs
- Criminal punishments for drug use/selling drugs
- Comparison of drug use to alcohol use in teens

<u>Activity #5</u>
Distribute the Non-fiction Assignment Sheet to students. Explain that students should choose a non-fiction topic related to *Go Ask Alice*. They should read a substantial article related to that topic and complete the Non-fiction Assignment Sheet for that article. Students may use magazines, newspapers, and the Internet as sources.

Activity #6
Bring the class back together and have each student tell what he/she read about.

Note: Compiling the Non-fiction Assignment Sheets into a booklet makes a nice follow-up activity and a handy reference for students.

Activity #7
Instruct students to find a poem about drugs. It can be about the death of someone on drugs, the pains of addiction, problems that have occurred while on drugs, or any other topic related to teenage drug use. If time remains allow students to use the library to find a poem. If not, have students find a poem on their own for homework. Tell students poems must be brought to class the next day.

NON-FICTION ASSIGNMENT SHEET
(To be completed after reading the required nonfiction article)

Name _____ Date _____

Title of Nonfiction Read _____

Written By _____ Publication Date _____

I. Factual Summary: Write a short summary of the piece you read.

II. Vocabulary
    1. With which vocabulary words in the piece did you encounter some degree of difficulty?

    2. How did you resolve your lack of understanding with these words?

III. Interpretation: What was the main point the author wanted you to get from reading his work?

IV. Criticism
    1. With which points of the piece did you agree or find easy to accept? Why?

    2. With which points of the piece did you disagree or find difficult to believe? Why?

V. Personal Response: What do you think about this piece? OR How does this piece influence your ideas?

LESSON FIVE

<u>Objectives</u>
1. To use poetry to make a connection with the novel
2. To discuss themes of the novel through various poems
3. To preview the vocabulary and study questions for Assignment 3
4. To read Assignment 3

<u>Activity #1</u>

Have students take out the poems they found relating to drug use. Distribute construction paper, scissors, glue, magazines, and newspapers. Have students write their poem on the construction paper. Next, tell them to find words and images that relate to the theme of their poem in the magazines and newspapers and place those items around the poem as a border.

<u>Activity #2</u>

After students have thought about the theme of their poem and found words and images to illustrate that theme, go around the room and have students read their poem to the class. The poems will be of a serious nature and should be making an impact on students, so try to make the transition from one reader to the next as simple and quick as possible. Be sure students are not only reading their poem, but also showing the words and images they selected to the class as well.

<u>Activity #3</u>

Once every student has shared his or her poem, ask students to reflect on all the poems that were just read. Have students write two short paragraphs– one discussing how they felt while trying to find images and words to illustrate the theme of their poem and one discussing the way they felt hearing all these poems read. After students have had 10-15 minutes to write their reflections, allow students to share what they wrote and discuss the impact of the poems. Ask students to talk about how these poems have allowed them to see a different perspective or have added insight to the events taking place in the novel. Also ask students to connect these themes with their own lives.

> Note: You may want to take some of the most powerful illustrated poems and hang them around your classroom.

<u>Activity #4</u>

Review the study questions and vocabulary for Assignment 3 orally together in class. Tell students that they should read Assignment 3 prior to the next class period. Give them the remainder of this class (if time remains) to complete this assignment.

LESSON SIX

Objectives
1. To bring ideas from the book into real life
2. To inform students about teenage drug use

Activity #1

This day is set aside for a guest speaker. Invite one or more of the following people from your community to speak to your class:

- Someone who has overcome a battle with drugs
- Police officer that deals with runaways and teenage drug cases
- Doctor that can discuss the affects of drugs on a person's health
- Spokesperson from a drug crisis/rehabilitation center
- Spokesperson from a drug prevention center
- Any other person that could educate your students about teenage drug use
- Therapist/Psychologist to talk about communication between teens and parents

Divide your class time according to how many speakers you're able to acquire. Remember to allow time for students to ask questions. Let each speaker know how much time he/she will have for the presentation. Allow for time at the end of the class for students to make connections with what they have learned from the speakers with what they have read in *Go Ask Alice*.

Follow Up: Be sure you and your students write thank you notes to each of your guests. At the very least, get a thank you card for each guest and have each of your students sign it (with any personal responses, if there is room).

LESSON SEVEN

Objectives
1. To review main ideas, events, and vocabulary of Assignment 3
2. To continue working on the time line
3. To preview study questions and vocabulary for Assignment 4
4. To read Assignment 4
5. To evaluate students' oral reading

Activity #1
    Have students answer the study guide questions for Assignment 3 as previously directed. Preview the questions for Assignment 4 while you have the study guides out.

Activity #2
    Review the answers to the Vocabulary Worksheet for Assignment 3. Make sure students write down the correct answers.

Activity #3
    Add events from the reading to the time line as previously described.

Activity #4
    Do the vocabulary worksheet for Assignment 4 together in class.

Activity #5
    Have students read assignment 4 of *Go Ask Alice* out loud in class. You probably know the best way to get readers with your class; pick students at random, ask for volunteers, or use whatever method works best for your group. If you have not yet completed an oral reading evaluation for your students, this would be a good opportunity to do so. A form is included with this unit for your convenience.

ORAL READING EVALUATION *Go Ask Alice*

Name _____ Class_____ Date _____

SKILL	EXCELLENT	GOOD	AVERAGE	FAIR	POOR
Fluency	5	4	3	2	1
Clarity	5	4	3	2	1
Audibility	5	4	3	2	1
Pronunciation	5	4	3	2	1
_____	5	4	3	2	1
_____	5	4	3	2	1

Total _____ Grade _____

Comments:

LESSON EIGHT

Objectives
1. To review main ideas, events, and vocabulary of Assignment 4
2. To continue working on the time line
3. To have students to assess the current anti-drug campaigns
4. To allow students to create newer, more effective anti-drug campaigns

Activity #1
Have students answer the study questions for reading Assignment 4 as previously directed.

Activity #2
Review the answers to the Vocabulary Worksheet for Assignment 4. Make sure students write down the correct answers.

Activity #3
Add events from the reading to the time line as previously described.

Activity #4
Show students anti-drug campaigns from the last few years. Initiate a class discussion about which anti-drug campaigns are the most effective and why. Discuss ideas on what could be done to reach teenagers today and educate them about the dangers of drug use. Included is a short list of websites that will allow you to view current anti-drug campaigns. You may also want to show some of the older drug campaigns to show how they have evolved (YouTube.com has several of the old "this is your brain" commercials). Check out a laptop and projector from your school resource center to view the videos and other materials with your students.

What's your anti-drug: http://www.whatsyourantidrug.com/
National Youth Anti-Drug Campaign: http://www.mediacampaign.org/mg/television.html
The Anti-Drug: http://www.theantidrug.com/
Above the Influence: http://www.abovetheinfluence.com
Not Even Once: http://www.notevenonce.com/

Activity #5
Place students into groups of four or five. Tell students they will be creating an anti-drug campaign of their own. Inform students that they will get time over the next few days to work together on their anti-drug campaign. Each group should create two large posters (that are different) that contain their campaign slogan. Students should also write a script for a TV commercial. Students should be prepared to perform their commercial, with any necessary props that are school appropriate, in front of the class on the due date. If possible, obtain a camcorder from your resource center to tape students as they perform their TV commercial for the class. Ask permission to hang the posters around school and play the commercials on your school news program. Give students the remainder of class time to work in their groups.

LESSON NINE

Objectives
1. To give students the opportunity to practice writing to persuade
2. To improve students' overall writing ability
3. To connect ideas and facts learned from the speaker and book with a real-life situation
4. To preview study questions and vocabulary for Assignment 5
5. To read Assignment 5

Activity #1
Since students have had a guest speaker discussing teen drug use and have read about Alice's battle with drugs, students should now be ready to write a persuasive essay on the subject. This persuasive essay will require students to convince a friend who is using drugs to stop and get the help he or she needs. Distribute Writing Assignment #2 to your students and use the Writing Evaluation Form included in this unit to provide feedback.

Activity #2
Review the study questions and vocabulary for Assignment 5 orally together in class. Tell students that they should read Assignment 5 prior to the next class period.

WRITING ASSIGNMENT #2 – *Go Ask Alice*
Writing to Persuade

PROMPT
Alice battles with her addiction to drugs throughout the novel, destroying her life in many ways and building a long list of regrets. Your assignment is to write a letter to persuade a close friend to stop using drugs and get the help he or she needs.

PREWRITING
Using your notes/information from the speaker and non-fiction assignment, create a list of reasons why someone should stop using drugs. Try to include facts and statistics for additional support. Include examples from the text on your list as well. Once you have created a list of reasons why your friend should stop using drugs, brainstorm a list of ways to get help. You will want to include ways to communicate with parents and how to complete the process for help.

DRAFTING
Write an introductory paragraph that addresses your friend and his or her problem. Express your concern for his or her well being and begin to explain why drugs are harmful in his or her life.

In the body paragraphs, continue to outline your reasons for wanting your friend to get help. Remember to use your facts, statistics, and examples from the text to support your view. Make each new reason a separate paragraph. After you have outlined the reasons why your friend should stop using drugs, begin to offer suggestions on how to get help.

In your concluding paragraph, make your final plea to your friend. Try to be supportive and sympathetic, while using a strong fact or example to leave the reader with a powerful ending.

PROMPT
When you finish the rough draft of your composition, ask a student who sits near you to read it. After reading your rough draft, he/she should tell you what he/she liked best about your work, which parts were difficult to understand, and ways in which your work could be improved. Reread your paper considering your critic's comments, and make the corrections you think are necessary. Ask your classmate what he/she thought of each of the characters/events you chose for your assignment.

PROOFREADING
Do a final proofreading of your paper double-checking your grammar, spelling, organization, and the clarity of your ideas.

WRITING EVALUATION FORM - *Go Ask Alice*

Name _____ Date _____

Writing Assignment # _____   Grade _____

Circle One For Each Item:

Introduction:	excellent	good	fair	poor
Body Paragraphs:	excellent	good	fair	poor
Conclusion:	excellent	good	fair	poor
Grammar:	excellent	good	fair	poor
Spelling:	excellent	good	fair	poor
Punctuation:	excellent	good	fair	poor
Legibility:	excellent	good	fair	poor
Persuasiveness:	excellent	good	fair	poor
_____	excellent	good	fair	poor

Strengths:

Weaknesses:

Comments/Suggestions:

LESSON TEN

<u>Objectives</u>
1. To review main ideas, events, and vocabulary of Assignment 5
2. To continue working on the time line
3. To allow students to create newer, more effective anti-drug campaigns

<u>Activity #1</u>
Have students answer the study guide questions for reading Assignment 5 as previously directed.

<u>Activity #2</u>
Review the answers to the Vocabulary Worksheet for Assignment 5. Make sure students write down the correct answers.

<u>Activity #3</u>
Add events from the reading to the time line as previously described.

<u>Activity #4</u>
With the remaining time allow students to get into their groups to work on their anti-drug campaign. Remind students that they need a slogan, two different posters, and a script for a TV commercial.

LESSON ELEVEN

Objectives
1. To bring ideas from the book into real life
2. To allow students to discover effective ways to communicate with parents

Activity #1

Throughout the book Alice continuously writes about how desperate she is to have someone to talk to about her drug problem. She is always wishing she could talk to her parents, but feels they wouldn't understand or that they would worry about her even more. Instead, Alice keeps her questions, feelings, and struggles inside, making her problems even worse.

Begin this activity by holding a class discussion on communication between teenagers and parents. Ask students to talk about their own relationships with their parents, pointing out what specifically is difficult for teenagers and parents in effective communication. Transition the discussion to talk about Alice's problems in talking with her parents. Brainstorm a list of examples in the novel when Alice is wishing she could talk to her parents.

Activity #2

After the discussion, break students into groups of four. Tell students they will be conducting a daytime talk show with Alice and her parents as the guests. Have each group select a famous talk show (Oprah, Dr. Phil, Maury, Montel, Greg Behrendt, etc) and determine who in the group will play the host, Alice, Alice's mother, and Alice's father. Once students have determined roles, have them begin to write a script. Encourage students to think about the format of most daytime talk shows and use that as their guide. Tell students to remain as close to the text and true personality of their character they are playing as possible. Remind students that the point of the assignment is to create and model effective communication between Alice and her parents. You may also want to remind students to keep the material school appropriate.

Once students have had time to write a short script, allow each group to host their talk show before the class. Afterwards, have students rate how well each group did in portraying effective communication between Alice and her parents.

LESSON TWELVE

Objectives
1. To give students the opportunity to practice writing to inform
2. To improve students' overall writing ability
3. To allow students to create newer, more effective anti-drug campaigns

Activity #1

Distribute the RAFT writing assignment to students. Explain that the purpose of this assignment is to write to inform. Tell students that they should select one of the scenarios listed for their third writing assignment. Explain that the "R" stands for the role they will take, or the point of view they are writing from; the "A" stands for the audience they are writing to; the "F" stands for the format of their writing; and the "T" stands for the topic or task. Quickly go over the different scenarios available to them and give the remaining time for students to complete the assignment.

Note: As students complete this writing assignment, call individuals up for writing conferences on the past two writing assignments. Use the evaluation form to guide you in your conference.

Activity #2

With the remaining time allow students to get into their groups to work on their anti-drug campaign. Inform students that this will be the last time they will have to work together on this campaign, and that any remaining work should be completed as homework.

Go Ask Alice Writing Assignment – RAFT

Directions: Select one of the following writing situations to use as the topic for your essay.

Role *The voice you take on as a writer; this is the perspective you are writing from*	Audience *Who you are writing to; this is the person that will be reading what you write*	Format *The form your writing will take; this is the type of writing you will complete*	Topic/Task *Your purpose for writing; this is the content or reason for your writing assignment*
Alice	Her parents	Speech	Explaining why she has trouble talking to them; confessing her problem with drugs
Joel	Alice	Email	Telling Alice how important it is she get help and offering tips on how to deal with her problems
Tim (Alice's brother)	Other students at his middle school	Newspaper Article	Explaining the dangers of drugs and why other students should stay away
You	Your parents	Letter	How you communicate; what can be done to improve communication

WRITING ASSIGNMENT #3 – *Go Ask Alice*
Writing to inform

PROMPT
Select one of the scenarios listed on the RAFT writing assignment for the topic of your essay. The role is the point of view you are writing from, the audience is who you are writing to, the format is the type of writing you are doing, and the topic/task is the actual information you are writing about.

PREWRITING
When you have selected your writing scenario, begin to brainstorm ideas. Remember to think about the role you are writing from and the topic you are writing about. Use your book, notes from the speaker, and notes from the non-fiction articles to help you with your support.

DRAFTING
Write an introductory paragraph that allows the reader to know the role you have assumed and the audience you are writing to. Give a general overview of the points you will make in the body paragraphs of your writing. Use the format of your writing to guide you on how to begin (speech would begin with a little about yourself, letter begins with Dear _____, etc).

In the body paragraphs, give the details of your topic. Use information from the novel, the speaker, and the non-fiction article you read to help provide support. Be sure to reread the topic/task you are writing on and be sure to cover all portions listed there.

In your conclusion paragraph, summarize your main points and conclude the writing assignment. For unity with your writing, you may want to tie in your role and audience once again.

PROMPT
When you finish the rough draft of your composition, ask a student who sits near you to read it. After reading your rough draft, he/she should tell you what he/she liked best about your work, which parts were difficult to understand, and ways in which your work could be improved. Reread your paper considering your critic's comments, and make the corrections you think are necessary. Ask your classmate what he/she thought of each of the characters/events you chose for your assignment.

PROOFREADING
Do a final proofreading of your paper double-checking your grammar, spelling, organization, and the clarity of your ideas.

WRITING EVALUATION FORM - *Go Ask Alice*

Name _____ Date _____

Writing Assignment # _____   Grade _____

Circle One For Each Item:

Introduction:	excellent	good	fair	poor
Body Paragraphs:	excellent	good	fair	poor
Conclusion:	excellent	good	fair	poor
Grammar:	excellent	good	fair	poor
Spelling:	excellent	good	fair	poor
Punctuation:	excellent	good	fair	poor
Legibility:	excellent	good	fair	poor
Quality of information/support:	excellent	good	fair	poor
_____	excellent	good	fair	poor

Strengths:

Weaknesses:

Comments/Suggestions:

LESSON THIRTEEN

<u>Objectives</u>
1. To allow students to share their anti-drug campaign
2. To raise awareness around the school about drug use
3. To help students make connections with the characters in the novel

<u>Activity #1</u>

Allow each group to present their anti-drug campaign. Try to obtain a camcorder to record the TV commercials as students perform them. If the school allows it, hang the posters around the school and air the commercials on the school news program.

<u>Activity #2</u>

As most students read the novel they recognized a date and connected it with meaning in their own lives. Instruct students to flip through the novel and pick out three dates in Alice's diary that hold meaning in their own lives (their birthday, friend or family member's birthday, important event, birth of sibling, etc). Have students create a double-entry journal where they write the date and what happened in Alice's life on the left side of the paper, with what happened in their life on the right side of the paper.

When students have had time to compare their life with dates in Alice's life, go around the room and ask students to share one of their examples. Hold a short discussion about perspective, talking about how different people have such drastically different things occurring on the same days. Ask students to think about looking at life from different perspectives and how on any given day someone could be experiencing complete happiness while others surrounding them are struggling with something difficult.

LESSONS FOURTEEN AND FIFTEEN

Objectives:
1. To allow students to experience the story of *Go Ask Alice* in a different medium
2. To get students to discuss the similarities and differences between the novel and the movie
3. To appreciate the qualities of both a novel and a movie

Activity #1

Purchase or rent the movie *Go Ask Alice*. The 1973 film version stars William Shatner and Andy Griffith. It can be purchased on Amazon.com or rented at Blockbuster or Netflix.

Prepare your students to watch the movie *Go Ask Alice*. Explain that even though the movie is based on the book, the two are not identical. Have students take notes of the similarities and differences they find while watching the video.

The video will take approximately two days to complete, depending on the length of your class.

Activity #2

When you have completed the video, hold a class discussion about the similarities and differences between the video and the novel. Talk about the qualities of both movies and novels, discussing the characteristics of each. Be sure to point out the things the producers did well when adapting the book into a movie, and things that can only be conveyed through original text. Allow students to decide which medium they enjoyed best with support for why they felt that way. Also allow students to discuss their feelings towards the actors and actresses selected for each role and how the movie was similar or different from what they have been picturing in their mind throughout the reading.

LESSON SIXTEEN

Objectives:
1. To discuss censorship and banned books
2. To practice debate skills

Activity #1

Ask your students to define censorship. Talk about censorship today (song lyrics, questionable magazine covers, television, etc) and allow students to voice their opinions about whether or not censorship in these areas is appropriate.

Transition the discussion to censorship and the novel. Provide students with examples of dates, places, and reasons why *Go Ask Alice* has been censored in the past.

> Because *Go Ask Alice* includes relatively explicit references to drugs and sex, conservative parents and activists have often sought to remove it from school libraries. Bans started in the 1970s: Kalamazoo in 1974, Saginaw in 1975, and Eagle Pass and Trenton in 1977 through removal from local libraries. Other libraries in New York (1975), Utah (1979), and Florida (1982) required parental permission for a student to check out the book. Additional bans occurred in 1983 in Minnesota and Colorado, 1984 in Mississippi, and 1986 in Georgia and Michigan. Also, in 1993 in New Jersey and West Virginia, 1994 in Massachusetts, 1998 in Rhode Island, and 2003 in Maine. The American Library Association listed *Go Ask Alice* as number 23 on its list of the 100 most frequently challenged books of the 1990s. The book was number 8 on the most challenged list in 2001 and up to number 6 in 2003.

Activity #2

Conduct a formal class debate on whether or not *Go Ask Alice* should be censored. Depending on the level of your students and their previous experience with debate, you may need to review or teach them the skills, rules, and procedures of a debate.

LESSONS SEVENTEEN AND EIGHTEEN

Objectives
1. To discuss the novel on a deeper than direct-recall level
2. To prepare students for questions and topics covered on the test
3. To allow students to make personal connection with the text

Activity #1

Choose the questions from the Extra Discussion Questions/Writing Assignments which seem most appropriate for your students. A class discussion of these questions is most effective if students have been given the opportunity to formulate answers to the questions prior to the discussion. To this end, you may either have all the students formulate answers to all the questions, divide your class into groups and assign one or more questions to each group, or you could assign one question to each student in your class. The option you choose will make a difference in the amount of class time needed for this activity.

Note: The use of graphic organizers may be helpful to students in preparing their answers. Encourage them to use any diagrams or graphics that they feel are necessary.

Activity #2

After reviewing the extra discussion questions, collect the reflective diary project assigned to students on the first day of the unit. Ask if any students would like to share any special parts of their projects with the class. Allow ample time for those who do want to share.

EXTRA DISCUSSION QUESTIONS/WRITING ASSIGNMENTS
Go Ask Alice

Interpretive
1. What are the main conflicts in the story? Describe each fully.

2. What is the setting, and what does it add to the story?

3. Describe the author's writing style. Give specific examples to support your answer.

4. List five of Alice's most important character traits and give examples of each.

5. From what point of view is the story told? Why is that important?

6. How does the editor keep people and places in the story anonymous?

7. How does the lack of dialogue affect the quality of the book?

Critical
8. Why does the book contain blank places in some sentences (-------------)?

9. What inferences can you make regarding the relationship Alice has with her mother at the beginning of the book?

10. How does Alice feel about fitting in with her family?

11. Alice says she feels like Alice in Wonderland. How is this allusion to the popular book and movie significant?

12. What is it about drugs that appeal to Alice? How does she change when she gets high?

13. Alice feels like her parents are disappointed with her and that she can't make them proud. Do you think her parents are truly disappointed with her, or are these feelings in her head? Explain your answer.

14. What similarities in home life do Chris and Alice have?

15. Alice's parents meet Richie and think he is a clean-cut gentleman. How do appearances that parents see differ from the real personalities of most teenagers?

16. What do the diary entries with a "?" mean?

17. How is Alice naive when it comes to her boyfriend Richie?

Go Ask Alice Extra Discussion Questions page 2

18. Alice says, "I'm getting more and more homesick every day instead of more weaned away." If she feels so sad in San Francisco, why doesn't she just go back home?

19. Alice and Chris visit her boss, Mr. Mellani, at his house for a family dinner. Compare and contrast his family and the way they interact with the way Alice and her family interact.

20. Alice and Chris dream of owning their own store, but when they finally own a successful shop, they aren't happy. Discuss the differences in the dreams the two girls had for their shop with the realities they face as shop owners.

21. Alice doesn't quite believe in a lot of the opinions the kids from Berkeley hold but says, "Maybe they'll wear me down to their way of thinking." What does this say about Alice's character?

22. After returning from California, Alice really loves and appreciates Christmas with her family. Why is this?

23. Alice's mother thinks Alice is finally back to her old life when she begins getting phone calls from old friends and going out on the weekends. How is this sense of comfort false?

24. Why does Alice think about giving her little brother a piece of candy with drugs on it?

25. Why does Alice run away from home for a second time? What conflicts does she have with her parents that make her want to leave?

26. Compare and contrast the home life Doris comes from to the home Alice left.

27. Alice says, "Everybody's been storytelling except me. I don't have any stories worth telling. All I can do is draw pictures of monsters and internal organs and hate." What does this mean?

28. What does Alice's new diary symbolize?

29. Alice begins to talk to people in Southern California about why they ran away from home. She tries to find a common thread that makes kids want to leave their parents. Ultimately, she finds out that hair is something kids and parents argue about all the time. What does the argument over hair really mean?

30. What do you think Alice's brother and sister go through as she battles drugs? How do you think they react to the situation and deal with what is going on in their home?

Go Ask Alice Extra Discussion Questions page 3

31. When Alice first gets back home she has an episode where her mind is out of her control, showing her a mix of past memories and creating new hallucinations. What might be the cause of this episode?

32. Alice says, "I used to think I was the only one who felt things, but I really am only one infinitely small part of an aching humanity. It's a good thing most people bleed on the inside or this would be a gory, blood-smeared earth." What does she mean?

33. How is Joel a positive person for Alice to have in her life? How does he help her grow as an individual?

34. Alice listens to Babbie tell how she became addicted to drugs. Babbie says at one point the school called her home to tell her parents she had been absent a lot. She told her father that it wasn't true, and that the school was so large they couldn't keep track of who was there and who wasn't. Alice says, "I don't know why her father believed that one, but I guess he did. It was probably too much trouble not to." What does Alice mean by that statement?

35. Does Alice get anything out of her group therapy? Explain your answer.

36. What does Alice discover about how most of the kids in the hospital feel about drug use?

37. Three weeks after Alice decides to stop keeping a diary she is found dead. What type of role did keeping a diary have in Alice's life? Did her choice to stop keeping a diary have anything to do with her death? Explain your answer.

38. In the epilogue it says, "Was it an accidental overdose? A premeditated overdose? No one knows, and in some ways that question isn't important." What does the editor mean when she says that how Alice died isn't important? What is important to know about her death?

Critical/Personal Response
39. Alice feels like all boys think about is sex; however, she feels that sex is something awkward and strange. How are girls and boys different when it comes to what they want out of dating and relationships?

40. Alice says that she doesn't feel like she can really be herself in front of her closest friends. She says, "I'm partly somebody else trying to fit in and say the right things and do the right thing and be in the right place and wear what everybody is wearing. Sometimes I think we're all trying to be shadows of each other." Do you think this is how teenagers are, always trying to fit in? Explain your answer. Compare and contrast the way Alice feels while around her friends with the way you feel when around your friends.

Go Ask Alice Extra Discussion Questions page 4

41. Alice complains about how her mother treats her, but then says she wants to be like her when she is a mother. How can Alice resent her mother for so much and then want to be the same way with her child? What qualities does your own mother have that you wish to have when you are a parent?

42. Alice wishes she could talk to her mother about sex and other things going on in her life. She says, "I wish I could talk to my mother about things like this because I don't really believe a lot of the kids know what they are talking about, at least I can't believe all the stuff they tell me." Why do you think she has such difficulty talking to her mother about these issues? Do you think this is common with teenagers now? Explain your answer.

43. Alice says, "Boy, Mom would be proud of my thinking and attitude today. It's just too bad we can't communicate anymore. I remember being able to talk to her when I was little but it's as though we speak a different language now and the meanings just don't come across the right way. She means something and I take it another way or she says something and I think she's trying to correct me or "uplift" me or preach at me and I really suspect she isn't doing that at all, just groping and being as lost with words as am I." Does this lack of communication between parents and teenagers happen often? Why do you think this is? What could be down to mend the communication gap?

44. Alice is glad that she was given drugs without her knowledge because she can feel "free and honest and virtuous" about not having made the choice herself. However, she still acknowledges that the high was exciting and that she was lucky to have gotten a soda with LSD. Do you think she has the right to feel honest and virtuous when she enjoyed the drug, even though she didn't choose to take it? Explain your answer.

45. Alice says, "I hereby solemnly promise that I will from this very day forward live so that everyone I know can be proud of me and so that I can be proud of myself!" Alice has high expectations for herself. Is she living up to the person she keeps telling herself she wants to be? Talk about a time in your life when you had difficulty living up to your own expectations.

46. Alice thinks that her family and friends would be mortified if they knew about her drug and sexual behavior but admits that they couldn't be more mortified than she is already. If Alice is so upset with her life and the choices she has made, then why does she continue to do the same things?

47. When thinking about losing her virginity to Bill, someone she didn't even care about, Alice says, "All my life I've thought that the first time I had sex with someone it would be something special." Is Alice's drug use compromising her own hopes and dreams? How do you think she will feel about this later in her life?

Go Ask Alice Extra Discussion Questions page 5

48. Alice feels like even at her young age she has already experienced so much. She says, "I just turned 15 and I can't stop life and get off." Do you think this is a common feeling for teenagers? Do you ever feel like this? Explain your answer.

49. Alice thinks about getting Roger to try drugs without his knowledge so he will understand what she feels like when she takes drugs. Do you think this is how teenagers often get started on drugs? Do you think Alice will feel better about herself if she can get others to do drugs, too? Explain your answer.

50. Alice and her parents have a serious discussion about her attitude. She says, "And they talked and talked and talked, but never once did they even hear one thing I was trying to say to them…I had the overwhelming desire to break down and tell them everything. I wanted to tell them! I wanted more than anything in the world to know that they understood, but naturally they just kept on talking and talking because they are incapable of really understanding anything. If only parents would listen!" Is this a common problem between parents and teenagers? How could this situation of understanding and listening be improved between parents and teenagers?

51. When Alice leaves to go to San Francisco she says, "I really am leaving mostly because I love you [her parents] so much and I don't want you to ever know what a weak and disreputable person I have been." Alice says she is leaving to save her parents from knowing what she does. Do you think the motivation behind her choice to leave is her parents, or is it just easier for Alice to leave town and avoid telling her parents about her problems? Explain your answer.

52. At Shelia's party, Alice and Chris become involved in the drug scene once again. Alice feels bad about it, but feels better knowing that this time she was an adult. Does moving to a new city and living on her own make her an adult? Explain your answer.

53. Alice is always saying the consequences that go with drugs are too high for anyone to pay. If she is constantly realizing the dangers and downfalls of drugs, why does she continue to go back to using each chance she gets?

54. Alice sounds upset about leaving Mr. Mellani a "thanks" and "I love you" note like she did her parents. Why do you think Alice leaves these notes instead of saying goodbye face to face?

55. Alice commits to not doing drugs several times throughout the novel. Despite how hard she tries, she still falls back to using drugs. Do you think the situations she puts herself in and the people she associates with influence her use of drugs? Use details from the text to support your answer.

Go Ask Alice Extra Discussion Questions page 6

56. Alice says, "Anyone who says pot and acid are not addicting is a damn, stupid, raving idiot, unenlightened fool! I've been on them since July 10, and when I've been off I've been scared to death to even think of anything that even looks or seems like dope. All the time pretending to myself that I could take it or leave it!" If Alice recognizes that she truly is addicted and can't take it or leave it, then why doesn't she get help?

57. Alice hates her life while living on the streets of Oregon and says, "Oh hell, I wish I had enough of anything to end the whole shitty mess." If Alice hates her life on drugs to the point she wishes she would die, why doesn't she get help? What would you do in Alice's situation?

58. Alice has always asked God for help in her life, yet becomes a "priestess of Satan" while living in Southern California. What do you think of her religious convictions? Is she as religious as she says throughout the book? Use details from the text to support your answer.

59. Alice meets a pregnant drug user who tells her that everyone will share the baby. What type of life will this child probably have?

60. Several other drugs users confess to Alice that they wished they could go back home. Most of the runaways feel like they can't go back home without giving up their identity. What do these teenagers mean when they say this? Do you think this is a valid excuse?

61. Alice talks about becoming a guidance counselor or a psychologist when she is older. She feels like she will be able to really understand what other teenagers are going through since she experienced it herself. Do you think Alice would be a good counselor? What qualities does she have that could help her in this role? What qualities does she have that might hurt her in this role?

62. Alice makes the decision to stop using drugs and get her life in order. She says she doesn't like the life drugs bring and that she doesn't like the drugs either. Do you think this is true? Does Alice really not like that life and feelings drugs bring? Explain your answer.

63. Alice says, "Every day for the rest of my life I shall dread weakening again and becoming something I simply do not want to be! I'll have to fight it every day of my life." Aside from drugs, what other things in life can haunt a teenager for years to come?

64. Alice feels like her parents are too protective and doesn't agree with a lot of their rules. Considering Alice's heavy drug use, do you think that her parents are justified in their rules? Do you think your parents have rules that may be annoying but are really there to help protect you? Give examples of rules your parents have that bother you, but when looked at from a different prospective can really protect you.

Go Ask Alice Extra Discussion Questions page 7

65. When Alice is with her father at the university she hears a professor giving statistics about how drug use, disease, and pregnancy in teens is on the rise. She reacts by thinking, "I really don't think the kids can be blamed for screwing up, at least not entirely. The adults don't seem to be doing much better." Do you think the problems of teenagers are a reflection of their parents and the way they are raised? Use details from the text and your own experiences in life to support your answer.

66. Do you think it's a good decision for Alice to avoid telling Joel the truth about her past? Why or why not?

67. Alice is afraid for her life because of the threats she has been getting from angry kids at school. Do you think she has a right to be that scared? Explain your answer using examples from the text and your experiences in life for support.

68. Alice doesn't tell her parents about the serious threats she is getting from kids at school. She also chooses not to tell them about the guy who grabbed her in the park and threatened her. Should she tell her parents? Would they understand?

69. Alice talks about her high school being divided into several cliques. She says that the students in those cliques seem to know nothing about anyone in another group. Compare and contrast this description of Alice's high school to your own.

70. While Alice is in the hospital healing she admits in her diary that she still has nightmares about the worms, but is keeping it to herself and not telling anyone. Do you think this is a good idea? Explain why or why not.

71. Though Alice never says who covered the peanuts with bad acid, the reader has a pretty good idea of who did it. Who do you think put Alice on a bad acid trip? What clues from the text support your reasoning?

72. Dr. Miller tells Alice that only she can help herself get better. He tells her that before she can begin to overcome her problem she has to admit she has a problem. Alice then thinks, "How could I do that when I really haven't [a problem]." Do you think Alice has a problem? Explain your answer.

73. Alice begins to listen to the stories of several of the drug addicted teenagers in the mental hospital. In almost each situation, the parent either suspected there was a problem but didn't deal with it or ignored the signs that something was wrong. Why do you think the parents in these situations acted the way they did? How do your parents handle problems with you? What method would you suggest to parents in dealing with teenagers?

74. Alice writes in her diary, "I know I couldn't exist without you." How has keeping a diary helped Alice? How is writing an outlet in your life?

Go Ask Alice Extra Discussion Questions page 8

75. At group therapy Alice is approached by Carter, the president of the group. Alice writes that he told her to, "Bring my thoughts and angers and fears out in the open to be examined. He told me that clumped inside they all seemed magnified and distorted out of true proportion." Do you believe this is true? Why or why not? How do you deal with your own problems in life?

76. Alice's father finally gets her released from the mental hospital and brings her home. Do you think Alice had worked through all her issues and was ready to be released? Explain your answer.

77. At the end of the diary Alice was preparing to start school. It would have been very easy for her to get wrapped up in drugs once again and accidentally overdose. On the other hand, Alice mentions death as an escape from her past and her problems several times throughout the novel, meaning the overdose could have been premeditated. How do you think Alice died? Use evidence from the text to support your answer.

Personal Response

78. Alice buys her diary as a way to express her most personal thoughts. She says, "I bought this diary because I thought at last I'd have something wonderful and great and worthwhile to say, something so personal that I wouldn't be able to share it with another living person, only myself." How do you share your most personal thoughts?

79. Alice says that her books are a part of her. She says, "I'm not really sure which parts of myself are real and which parts are things I've gotten from books." Does this ever happen to you? Do you see parts of books, movies, music, or television shows in parts of you? Explain your answer.

80. Alice believes that Roger is her one and only true love. She can't imagine another guy ever touching her or loving her, and vows never to be with anyone else. Do you agree that she found her true love in high school? Do you think that these feelings are similar to what high school students feel today? Explain your answer.

81. Alice is excited to move to a new city, but is also nervous about leaving her home. She points out that she has lived in that house her whole life and that many of her memories take place there. How would you feel if your parents told you the family was moving? What about moving would be hardest for you?

82. Alice has heard horror stories about people who use drugs; however, she is very curious to see how other drugs can make her feel. Do you think curiosity overpowers knowledge and rational thinking when it comes to experimenting with drugs? Why do you think this is?

Go Ask Alice Extra Discussion Questions page 9

83. Alice says, "All the things I heard about LSD were obviously written by uniformed, ignorant people like my parents who obviously don't know what they're talking about." Do parents, teachers, law enforcement officers, and the media accurately portray drugs? How should these sources explain drug use and the consequences to teenagers in a way that would be most effective?

84. When Alice's grandfather has a heart attack she begins to think about death and what happens to a person's soul. What do you think happens when a person dies?

85. When talking about being friends with the popular crowd Alice says, "I was so pleased and felt so smart when they accepted me and now I feel miserable and ashamed." Do you think teenagers compromise who they are to be accepted by others? Explain your answer. What have you done to gain friendship or acceptance that later made you feel ashamed?

86. Alice gets homesick and misses her family while she is away, but feels like she can't call them. If you were in Alice's situation, what would you do?

87. Alice feels trapped in the drug scene and can't escape it. If you were in Alice's situation, what would you do to get your life back in order?

88. Alice says, "Adolescents have a very rocky insecure time. Grown-ups treat them like children and yet expect them to act like adults. They give them orders like little animals, then expect them to react like mature, and always rational, self-assured persons of legal stature. It is a difficult, lost, vacillating time." Do you agree with Alice's statement? How does it relate to your life?

89. Alice makes a New Year's resolution to change her life and stay away from drugs. What New Year's resolutions have you made in the past few years? Have you kept any of them? Describe the difficulty in keeping resolutions.

90. Alice wrestles with her addiction to drugs while telling herself she can stop anytime. Do you think people who use drugs can truly stop using when they want to? Explain your answer.

91. Alice comes from a really supportive and caring family, while many of her other friends who use drugs have come from abusive homes. Do you think there is any one type of person that gets hooked on drugs, or can it happen to anyone? Explain your answer.

92. Alice says, "I just wish I could love myself." Do you think teenagers often have a difficult time loving who they really are? Have you ever had a hard time loving yourself?

Go Ask Alice Extra Discussion Questions page 10

93. Several of the drug users in the novel struggle with their parents over freedom, identity, and power of decision. How do you handle these same issues in your own family?

94. Alice says, "I have just read the stuff I wrote in the last few weeks and I am being drowned in my own tears…I could never have done things like that!" What have you done in your life that surprised you? How did you work to move on from your actions and live your life?

95. Alice's grandpa tells her she only has to forgive herself. Why is forgiving yourself such a hard thing to do? When have you had trouble forgiving yourself for your actions?

96. The diary entries that Alice writes when she is discovering her injuries in the first few days at the hospital are very descriptive in terms of the damage she did to herself. How did you feel as you were reading these entries?

97. Alice says that the school at the mental hospital is a privilege that must be earned. What do you think about school being a privilege? Should an education be something earned by good behavior, or should everyone be entitled to it no matter what? Explain your answer.

98. Alice wonders if her mother had ever kissed another guy before her father. What do you think your parents were like when they were your age?

99. Alice says, "I have this very silly fear, dear friend, that one day I'll be old, without ever having really been young. I wonder if it could happen that quickly or if I've ruined my life already. Do you think life can get by you without your ever seeing it?" What do you think about this idea?

100. How did you feel after reading the epilogue? Where you surprised by the outcome of the story?

101. Alice chose to use drugs for several reasons. Analyze her motivation throughout the book to use drugs. Give at least three reasons Alice felt the need to use drugs. Are these reasons things that teenagers deal with in their lives today?

102. Alice's decision to use drugs ultimately leads to her death. Think about how the choices you make while in high school can affect the rest of your life. How do you deal with the bad decisions you make in your lifetime? Are the choices that you make now something that will haunt you later in life? Give examples to support your answer.

103. Some people say that in order to really learn something you have to experience it yourself. Others argue that seeing something happening to someone else serves as an effective warning. What do you think? Do you think the editor achieved her goal of trying to warn teenagers to stay away from drugs? Do you think the editor achieved her goal with you?

Go Ask Alice Extra Discussion Questions page 11

104. Throughout the book Alice struggles with wanting to tell her parents what is going on. Knowing that deep down Alice really wanted help despite how she acted towards her family and friends, and knowing how devastating drugs can be, how would you handle this problem if one of your friends was using drugs? How would you handle this problem if you were a parent and your child was beginning to use drugs?

QUOTATIONS - *Go Ask Alice*

1. "I guess I just can't be secure no matter what happens." December 22

2. "Oh dear God, help me adjust, help me be accepted, help me belong, don't let me be a social outcast and a drag on my family." January 1

3. "I really do love Tim and Alex, but they've got plenty of faults too, and I find it difficult to decide whether I love them more than I hate them or whether I hate them more than I love them. This also applies to Mom and Dad! But truthfully I guess it applies even more to myself." April 20

4. "For the first time that I could remember in my whole life, I was completely uninhibited." July 10

5. "I danced like I have never dreamed possible for introverted, mousy little me. I felt great, free, abandoned, a different, improved, perfected specimen of a different, improved, perfected species." July 20

6. "I don't know why I shouldn't use drugs, because they're wild and they're beautiful and they're wonderful, but I know I shouldn't, and I won't! I won't ever again. I hereby solemnly promise that I will from this very day forward live so that everyone I know can be proud of me and so that I can be proud of myself!" July 23

7. "All my life I've thought that the first time I had sex with someone it would be something special, and maybe even painful, but it turned out to be just a part of the brilliant, freaky, way-out, forever pattern." August 6

8. "Oh, how I wish I had someone, anyone, to talk with who knows what they're talking about." August 6

9. "I'm living with doubts and apprehensions and fears that I never dreamed possible." August 7

10. "It's all I can do to keep from crying. Mom and Dad just called to say how proud they are to have me for a daughter. There are no words to express how I feel." August 13

11. "I'm afraid to live and afraid to die, just like the old Negro spiritual." August 14

12. "Everyone is terribly worried about me and, in fact, I'm even terribly worried about myself, ..." August 16

13. "But they [parents] won't listen! They simply won't or can't or don't want to listen, and we kids keep winding up back in the same old frustrating, lost, lonely corner with no one to relate to either verbally or physically." September 7

Go Ask Alice Quotations Page 2

14. "I really am leaving mostly because I love you [her parents] so much and I don't want you to ever know what a weak and disreputable person I have been." Unknown date

15. "I will never ever, ever, under any circumstances use drugs again. They are the root and cause of this whole rotten, stinking mess I am in, and I wish with all my heart and soul that I had never heard of them." November 5

16. "We've had it! The garbage that goes with drugs makes the price too goddamned high for anyone to pay." December 3

17. "I'm lonely, I'm heartbroken, I hate this whole number and everything it stands for, I feel I'm wasting my life away. I want to go back to my family and school." December 18

18. "Anyone who says pot and acid are not addicting is a damn, stupid, raving idiot, unenlightened fool! I've been on them since July 10, and when I've been off I've been scared to death to even think of anything that even looks or seems like dope. All the time pretending to myself that I could take it or leave it!" January 24

19. "I haven't any clothes except these I had on when I left home and I'm getting so damned dirty I think they've grown on me…I've got a fucking head cold and I feel miserable, and my period has started and I don't have any Tampax." Unknown date

20. ". . . I've got a fever and I'm dripping wet and so filthy and smelly I can hardly stand myself." Unknown date

21. "I'm scared and lonely and I'm sick. I'm as sick as I've ever been in my life." Unknown date

22. "I'm actually and literally and completely sick to my stomach. I want to puke all over the shitty world. Most of the way down we rode with a big fat assed, baby screwing truck driver who picked us up and got his kicks by physically hurting Doris and watching her cry." Unknown date

23. "I can't understand how they [her parents] can possibly still love me and still want me but they do! They do!" Unknown date

24. "Wow! I am through with drugs too. I've used the hard stuff only a few times and I don't like it. I don't like any of it. The uppers or the downers. I'm through with the whole mess. Absolutely and completely and forever, really I am." Unknown date

Go Ask Alice Quotations Page 3

25. "I have two choices; I must either commit suicide or try to rectify my life by helping others." Unknown date

26. "Every day for the rest of my life I shall dread weakening again and becoming something I simply do not want to be! I'll have to fight it every day of my life and I hope God will help me."   April 6

27. "When I'm having the very nicest thoughts, the black ugly past comes flooding in like a nightmare." April 14

28. "I've even started praying every night like I used to when I was little, but now I'm not just saying words, I'm begging. I'm pleading." April 24

29. "For the first time I feel absolutely certain that even if I were locked in a room full of acid, Speed, and every other upper in the world I would only be disgusted, for I see what it does to kids who used to be my friends." June 10

30. "The whole ends of my fingers have been torn off and two nails have been pulled out completely and the others torn down almost in half…I can feel my face is all clawed up too, and my knees and feet and elbows, in fact most of my body is wrenched and battered and bruised…splints on four toes so I guess they are broken too…My face is puffed and swollen and black and blue and scratched, and my hair has been pulled out in big patches till I have completely bald areas." Unknown date

31. "All that kept running through my brain was I'm scared, I'm scared, I'm scared." July 23

32. "I'm so grateful for group therapy. Maybe now I'll get something out of this place instead of being broken by it." August 1

33. "I'm so very, very grateful that they [Alice's family] don't hate me, because in a lot of ways I hate myself." August 9

34. "Why can't we just be ourselves and have everyone accept us the way we are? Why can't I just be *me* as I am now and not have to concentrate and fume and get upset about my past and my future." September 19

LESSON NINETEEN

Objective
To review all of the vocabulary work done in this unit

Activity #1:
Choose one (or more) of the vocabulary review activities listed below and spend your class period as directed in the activity. Some of the materials for these review activities are located in the Vocabulary Resource Materials section in this LitPlan.

VOCABULARY REVIEW ACTIVITIES

1. Divide your class into two teams and have an old-fashioned spelling or definition bee.

2. Give each of your students (or students in groups of two, three or four) a *Go Ask Alice* Vocabulary Word Search Puzzle. The person (group) to find all of the vocabulary words in the puzzle first wins.

3. Give students a *Go Ask Alice* Vocabulary Word Search Puzzle without the word list. The person or group to find the most vocabulary words in the puzzle wins.

4. Use a *Go Ask Alice* Vocabulary Crossword Puzzle. Put the puzzle onto a transparency on the overhead projector (so everyone can see it), and do the puzzle together as a class.

5. Give students a *Go Ask Alice* Vocabulary Matching Worksheet to do.

6. Divide your class into two teams. Use *Go Ask Alice* vocabulary words with their letters jumbled as a word list. Student 1 from Team A faces off against Student 1 from Team B. You write the first jumbled word on the board. The first student (1A or 1B) to unscramble the word wins the chance for his/her team to score points. If 1A wins the jumble, go to student 2A and give him/her a definition. He/she must give you the correct spelling of the vocabulary word which fits that definition. If he/she does, Team A scores a point, and you give student 3A a definition for which you expect a correctly spelled matching vocabulary word. Continue giving Team A definitions until some team member makes an incorrect response. An incorrect response sends the game back to the jumbled-word face off, this time with students 2A and 2B. Instead of repeating giving definitions to the first few students of each team, continue with the student after the one who gave the last incorrect response on the team. For example, if Team B wins the jumbled-word face-off, and student 5B gave the last incorrect answer for Team B, you would start this round of definition questions with student 6B, and so on. The team with the most points wins!

7. Have students write a story in which they correctly use as many vocabulary words as possible. Have students read their compositions orally! Post the most original compositions on your bulletin board!

LESSON TWENTY

Objectives:
>To review the main ideas and events in *Go Ask Alice*

Activity #1:
Choose one of the review games/activities suggested below and spend your class time as directed there.

REVIEW GAMES/ACTIVITIES *Go Ask Alice*

1. Ask the class to make up a unit test for *Go Ask Alice*. The test should have 4 sections: matching, true/false, short answer, and essay. Students may use 1/2 period to make the test and then swap papers and use the other 1/2 class period to take a test a classmate has devised. (open book) You may want to use the unit test included in this packet or take questions from the students' unit tests to formulate your own test.

2. Take 1/2 period for students to make up true and false questions (including the answers). Collect the papers and divide the class into two teams. Draw a big tic-tac-toe board on the chalk board. Make one team X and one team O. Ask questions to each side, giving each student one turn. If the question is answered correctly, that students' team's letter (X or O) is placed in the box. If the answer is incorrect, no letter is placed in the box. The object is to get three in a row like tic-tac-toe. You may want to keep track of the number of games won for each team.

3. Take 1/2 period for students to make up questions (true/false and short answer). Collect the questions. Divide the class into two teams. You'll alternate asking questions to individual members of teams A & B (like in a spelling bee). The question keeps going from A to B until it is correctly answered, then a new question is asked. A correct answer does not allow the team to get another question. Correct answers are +2 points; incorrect answers are -1 point.

4. Have students pair up and quiz each other from their study guides and class notes.

5. Give students a *Go Ask Alice* crossword puzzle to complete.

6. Play What's My Line?. This is similar to the old television show. Students assume the roles of different characters from the epic. One student gives clues to the class, or to a panel of contestants. The contestants try to guess the identity of the guest. Students may enjoy assisting you in creating rules and procedures for the game.

7. Divide your class into two teams. Use *Go Ask Alice* crossword words with their letters jumbled as a word list. Student 1 from Team A faces off against Student 1 from Team B. You write the first jumbled word on the board. The first student (1A or 1B) to unscramble the word wins the chance for his/her team to score points. If 1A wins the jumble, go to student 2A and give him/her a clue. He/she must give you the correct word which matches that clue. If he/she does, Team A scores a point, and you give student 3A a clue for which you expect another correct response. Continue giving Team A clues until some team member makes an incorrect response. An incorrect response sends the game back to the jumbled-word face off, this time with students 2A and 2B. Instead of repeating

giving clues to the first few students of each team, continue with the student after the one who gave the last incorrect response on the team. For example, if Team B wins the jumbled-word face-off, and student 5B gave the last incorrect answer for Team B, you would start this round of clue questions with student 6B, and so on. The team with the most points wins!

8. Play Jeopardy. Divide the class into two groups. Assign each group a category or book from the epic and have them devise answers for that category. Play the game according to the television show procedures.

9. Play Drawing in the Details. This is similar to Pictionary. Divide students into teams. A student from one team draws a scene from the epic. (You may want to specify the Book or section.) Drawings should be kept simple, to keep the pace lively. Students in the opposing team locate the scene in their books and read it aloud. If they are incorrect, the illustrator's team has a chance to guess. Involve students in setting up a scoring system and any other necessary rules.

UNIT TESTS

SHORT ANSWER UNIT TEST 1 - *Go Ask Alice*

I. Matching/Identify

____ 1. Tim   A. Alice's favorite holiday

____ 2. Shrink   B. Person Alice envisions covered in maggots and worms

____ 3. New York   C. "Straight" girl who Alice is friends with

____ 4. Chris   D. Person judge orders Alice to see

____ 5. Jan   E. What Joel gives Alice while she is in the hospital

____ 6. Christmas   F. Alice thinks this is from Mr. Larsen

____ 7. Social Worker   G. Location of mission that helps Alice

____ 8. Alex   H. Boyfriend of Alice's that convinces her to start selling drugs

____ 9. Richie   I. Place Alice's parents take her to avoid peer pressure at school

____ 10. Denver   J. Shows up high while Alice is babysitting

____ 11. Letter   K. Friend Alice makes at the mental hospital

____ 12. Grandpa   L. How Alice thinks about giving her siblings drugs

____ 13. Marcie   M. Where Alice runs away the second time

____ 14. Mountains   N. Person Alice talks to about avoiding peer pressure and drugs

____ 15. Peanuts   O. Opens a boutique with Alice near Berkeley

____ 16. California   P. Alice's chosen career

____ 17. New Year's   Q. Alice's younger sister

____ 18. Candy   R. Lies to judge about Alice selling drugs

____ 19. Fawn   S. Place Alice visits with her mom while her dad substitutes

____ 20. Babbie   T. When Alice bonds with family while cleaning in her pajamas

Go Ask Alice Short Answer Unit Test 1 Page 2

II. Short Answer

1. Describe the game "Button, Button, Who's Got the Button."

2. Alice begins to sell drugs to help her boyfriend earn money. Who does she sell drugs to that makes her feel really guilty and upset?

3. What happens to Alice and Chris that makes them leave San Francisco?

4. How do other students react when Alice returns to school?

5. When Alice runs away a second time, she continues writing but not in her diary. What does she use instead?

6. How does Alice get money to buy drugs?

7. Why does Alice want to get a new diary when she gets back home?

8. What do the kids at school threaten to do to Alice's family?

9. Describe the physical condition Alice is in at the hospital.

10. What happens after Alice decides not to keep a diary?

Go Ask Alice Short Answer Unit Test 1 Page 3

III. Vocabulary
　　　　Write down the vocabulary words. Go back later and write down the correct definition for each word.

1.

2.

3.

4.

5.

6.

7.

8.

9.

10.

IV. Essay
Select *one* of the following topics and respond in an essay:

Alice begins to talk to people in Southern California about why they ran away from home. She tries to find a common thread that makes kids want to leave their parents. Ultimately, she finds out that hair is something kids and parents argue about all the time. What does the argument over hair really mean?

What did Alice's diary mean to her? Why was it important in her life?

SHORT ANSWER UNIT TEST 1 ANSWER KEY – *Go Ask Alice*

I. Matching/Identify

N	1. Tim	A.	Alice's favorite holiday
D	2. Shrink	B.	Person Alice envisions covered in maggots and worms
S	3. New York	C.	"Straight" girl who Alice is friends with
O	4. Chris	D.	Person judge orders Alice to see
J	5. Jan	E.	What Joel gives Alice while she is in the hospital
A	6. Christmas	F.	Alice thinks this is from Mr. Larsen
P	7. Social Worker	G.	Location of mission that helps Alice
Q	8. Alex	H.	Boyfriend of Alice's that convinces her to start selling drugs
H	9. Richie	I.	Place Alice's parents take her to avoid peer pressure at school
M	10. Denver	J.	Shows up high while Alice is babysitting
E	11. Letter	K.	Friend Alice makes at the mental hospital
B	12. Grandpa	L.	How Alice thinks about giving her siblings drugs
R	13. Marcie	M.	Where Alice runs away the second time
I	14. Mountains	N.	Person Alice talks to about avoiding peer pressure and drugs
F	15. Peanuts	O.	Opens a boutique with Alice near Berkeley
G	16. California	P.	Alice's chosen career
T	17. New Year's	Q.	Alice's younger sister
L	18. Candy	R.	Lies to judge about Alice selling drugs
C	19. Fawn	S.	Place Alice visits with her mom while her dad substitutes
K	20. Babbie	T.	When Alice bonds with family while cleaning in her pajamas

Go Ask Alice Short Answer Unit Test 1 Answer Key Page 2

II. Short Answer

1. Describe the game "Button, Button, Who's Got the Button."
    In this game a tray of fourteen sodas is brought out. Ten of the drinks contain the drug LSD. Ten "lucky" people get high, while the others babysit.

2. Alice begins to sell drugs to help her boyfriend earn money. Who does she sell drugs to that makes her feel really guilty and upset?
    Alice feels bad for selling drugs to elementary school students.

3. What happens to Alice and Chris that makes them leave San Francisco?
    Alice and Chris are raped by Shelia and her boyfriend while high one night.

4. How do other students react when Alice returns to school?
    Several kids approach Alice and harass her for drugs. She used to sell drugs and they don't believe that she has changed. Many of Alice's old friends try to get her to go to parties and be the person she was before she left.

5. When Alice runs away a second time, she continues writing but not in her diary. What does she use instead?
    Alice uses single sheets of paper, paper bags, and other items around her to write her diary entries.

6. How does Alice get money to buy drugs?
    Alice panhandles on the side of the road, begging people for money. She also performs sexual favors with strangers to get drugs.

7. Why does Alice want to get a new diary when she gets back home?
    Alice feels like her first diary is her past, her life on drugs. When she gets home she wants to start a new diary that will be her future, a life without drugs.

8. What do the kids at school threaten to do to Alice's family?
    The kids at school say they will get even for her calling Jan's mother. They threaten to give Alice's younger brother and sister candy laced with drugs. They also threaten to put drugs in her father's car to make him look bad and lose his job.

9. Describe the physical condition Alice is in at the hospital.
    Alice has torn off the tops of her fingers, she has missing fingernails, her face is scratched and clawed up, she is missing chunks of her hair and her scalp is exposed, her body is badly bruised, and several of her toes are broken. She also has a brain concussion.

Go Ask Alice Short Answer Unit Test 1 Answer Key Page 3

10. What happens after Alice decides not to keep a diary?
    Three weeks after Alice stops keeping a diary she is found dead from an overdose on drugs. No one knows whether or not it was accidently or premeditated.

III. Vocabulary
    Write down the vocabulary words. Go back later and write down the correct definition for each word.

1.

2.

3.

4.

5.

6.

7.

8.

9.

10.

IV. Essay

Grade the essay according to your own criteria.

Select *one* of the following topics and respond in an essay:

Alice begins to talk to people in Southern California about why they ran away from home. She tries to find a common thread that makes kids want to leave their parents. Ultimately, she finds out that hair is something kids and parents argue about all the time. What does the argument over hair really mean?

What did Alice's diary mean to her? Why was it important in her life?

SHORT ANSWER UNIT TEST 2 - *Go Ask Alice*

I. Matching/Identify

____ 1. Letter   A. Opens a boutique with Alice near Berkeley

____ 2. Peanuts   B. Alice's younger sister

____ 3. Marcie   C. Shows up high while Alice is babysitting

____ 4. Denver   D. Alice's favorite holiday

____ 5. Richie   E. Place Alice visits with her mom while her dad substitutes

____ 6. Babbie   F. How Alice thinks about giving her siblings drugs

____ 7. Christmas   G. "Straight" girl who Alice is friends with

____ 8. Fawn   H. Where Alice runs away the second time

____ 9. Mountains   I. Person Alice envisions covered in maggots and worms

____ 10. Candy   J. What Joel gives Alice while she is in the hospital

____ 11. Tim   K. When Alice bonds with family while cleaning in her pajamas

____ 12. Grandpa   L. Location of mission that helps Alice

____ 13. Alex   M. Boyfriend of Alice's that convinces her to start selling drugs

____ 14. New Year's   N. Alice thinks this is from Mr. Larsen

____ 15. Chris   O. Place Alice's parents take her to avoid peer pressure at school

____ 16. Jan   P. Lies to judge about Alice selling drugs

____ 17. Shrink   Q. Person Alice talks to about avoiding peer pressure and drugs

____ 18. Social Worker   R. Person judge orders Alice to see

____ 19. New York   S. Alice's chosen career

____ 20. California   T. Friend Alice makes at the mental hospital

Go Ask Alice Short Answer Unit Test 2 Page 2

II. Short Answer

1. Describe Alice's first high.

2. According to Alice's friend, why do more kids prefer drugs to alcohol?

3. After vowing to never do drugs again, Alice and Chris get mixed up in the drug scene in San Francisco. What event prompts the two friends to begin using drugs again?

4. Describe the shop Alice and Chris open near Berkeley.

5. When Alice runs away a second time, she continues writing but not in her diary. What does she use instead?

6. What do the people at the mission do for Alice?

7. Alice is worried that with all the sex she is having she may get pregnant. Why can't she take the birth control pill to protect herself?

8. How does Alice perform as a student when she returns to school after running away the second time?

9. How does Alice meet Joel?

10. Describe the physical condition Alice is in at the hospital.

Go Ask Alice Short Answer Unit Test 2 Page 3

III. Vocabulary

Write down the vocabulary words. Go back later and write down the correct definitions for the words.

1.

2.

3.

4.

5.

6.

7.

8.

9.

10.

IV. Essay

Select *one* of the following topics and respond in an essay:

Alice commits to not doing drugs several times throughout the novel. Despite how hard she tries, she still falls back to using drugs. Do you think the situations she puts herself in and the people she associates with influence her use of drugs? Use details from the text to support your answer.

In the epilogue it says, "Was it an accidental overdose? A premeditated overdose? No one knows, and in some ways that question isn't important." What does the editor mean when she says that how Alice died isn't important? What is important to know about her death?

SHORT ANSWER UNIT TEST 2 ANSWER KEY - *Go Ask Alice*

I. Matching/Identify

J	1. Letter	A.	Opens a boutique with Alice near Berkeley
N	2. Peanuts	B.	Alice's younger sister
P	3. Marcie	C.	Shows up high while Alice is babysitting
H	4. Denver	D.	Alice's favorite holiday
M	5. Richie	E.	Place Alice visits with her mom while her dad substitutes
T	6. Babbie	F.	How Alice thinks about giving her siblings drugs
D	7. Christmas	G.	"Straight" girl who Alice is friends with
G	8. Fawn	H.	Where Alice runs away the second time
O	9. Mountains	I.	Person Alice envisions covered in maggots and worms
F	10. Candy	J.	What Joel gives Alice while she is in the hospital
Q	11. Tim	K.	When Alice bonds with family while cleaning in her pajamas
I	12. Grandpa	L.	Location of mission that helps Alice
B	13. Alex	M.	Boyfriend of Alice's that convinces her to start selling drugs
K	14. New Year's	N.	Alice thinks this is from Mr. Larsen
A	15. Chris	O.	Place Alice's parents take her to avoid peer pressure at school
C	16. Jan	P.	Lies to judge about Alice selling drugs
R	17. Shrink	Q.	Person Alice talks to about avoiding peer pressure and drugs
S	18. Social Worker	R.	Person judge orders Alice to see
E	19. New York	S.	Alice's chosen career
L	20. California	T.	Friend Alice makes at the mental hospital

Go Ask Alice Short Answer Unit Test 2 Answer Key Page 2

II. Short Answer

1. Describe Alice's first high.
    Alice loses all her inhibitions. She experiences every sound, touch, and sight to the fullest. She really loves the feeling she has when high and feels happier and more carefree than ever before.

2. According to Alice's friend, why do more kids prefer drugs to alcohol?
    Alice's friend says that drugs are easier for teenagers to get than alcohol.

3. After vowing to never do drugs again, Alice and Chris get mixed up in the drug scene in San Francisco. What event prompts the two friends to begin using drugs again?
    Chris's boss, Shelia, invites the girls to a party at her house. Alice and Chris go to the party to find that people are passing around a joint. The girls can't resist and begin heavy drug use once again.

4. Describe the shop Alice and Chris open near Berkeley.
    Alice and Chris open a shop where college kids stop by to watch TV and sit around. There is a regular crowd and the business is fairly successful.

5. When Alice runs away a second time, she continues writing but not in her diary. What does she use instead?
    Alice uses single sheets of paper, paper bags, and other items around her to write her diary entries.

6. What do the people at the mission do for Alice?
    The people at the mission let Alice take a shower and give her some clean clothes and tampons. They feed her and take her to the doctor for her fever and try to talk to her about communicating with her parents.

7. Alice is worried that with all the sex she is having she may get pregnant. Why can't she take the birth control pill to protect herself?
    Alice uses so many drugs and blacks out so often that she can rarely tell what day it is. She can't take the pill for protection unless she can remember to take it each day, so she just hopes she doesn't end up pregnant.

8. How does Alice perform as a student when she returns to school after running away the second time?
    Alice becomes a very devoted student. She studies for several hours each night and gets very high grades in all her classes.

9. How does Alice meet Joel?
    Alice's dad gets special permission for her to use the university library. While she is there studying one afternoon she meets Joel, a student at the university.

Go Ask Alice Short Answer Unit Test 2 Answer Key Page 3

10. Describe the physical condition Alice is in at the hospital.
    Alice has torn off the tops of her fingers, she has missing fingernails, her face is scratched and clawed up, she is missing chunks of her hair and her scalp is exposed, her body is badly bruised, and several of her toes are broken. She also has a brain concussion.

III. Vocabulary

Write down the vocabulary words. Go back later and write down the correct definitions for the words.

1.

2.

3.

4.

5.

6.

7.

8.

9.

10.

IV. Essay
Select *one* of the following topics and respond in an essay:

Alice commits to not doing drugs several times throughout the novel. Despite how hard she tries, she still falls back to using drugs. Do you think the situations she puts herself in and the people she associates with influence her use of drugs? Use details from the text to support your answer.

In the epilogue it says, "Was it an accidental overdose? A premeditated overdose? No one knows, and in some ways that question isn't important." What does the editor mean when she says that how Alice died isn't important? What is important to know about her death?

ADVANCED SHORT ANSWER UNIT TEST *Go Ask Alice*

I. Matching/Identify

____ 1. Letter   A. Opens a boutique with Alice near Berkeley

____ 2. Peanuts   B. Alice's younger sister

____ 3. Marcie   C. Shows up high while Alice is babysitting

____ 4. Denver   D. Alice's favorite holiday

____ 5. Richie   E. Place Alice visits with her mom while her dad substitutes

____ 6. Babbie   F. How Alice thinks about giving her siblings drugs

____ 7. Christmas   G. "Straight" girl who Alice is friends with

____ 8. Fawn   H. Where Alice runs away the second time

____ 9. Mountains   I. Person Alice envisions covered in maggots and worms

____ 10. Candy   J. What Joel gives Alice while she is in the hospital

____ 11. Tim   K. When Alice bonds with family while cleaning in her pajamas

____ 12. Grandpa   L. Location of mission that helps Alice

____ 13. Alex   M. Boyfriend of Alice's that convinces her to start selling drugs

____ 14. New Year's   N. Alice thinks this is from Mr. Larsen

____ 15. Chris   O. Place Alice's parents take her to avoid peer pressure at school

____ 16. Jan   P. Lies to judge about Alice selling drugs

____ 17. Shrink   Q. Person Alice talks to about avoiding peer pressure and drugs

____ 18. Social Worker   R. Person judge orders Alice to see

____ 19. New York   S. Alice's chosen career

____ 20. California   T. Friend Alice makes at the mental hospital

Go Ask Alice Advanced Short Answer Unit Test Page 2

II. Short Answer

1. Why does the book contain blank places in some sentences (-------------) and question marks at the start of some entries?

2. Alice's parents meet Richie and think he is a clean-cut gentleman. Her mother describes other friends of hers as "nice girls." How do appearances that her parents see differ from the real personalities of her friends?

3. Alice's mother thinks Alice is finally back to her old life when she begins getting phone calls from old friends and going out on the weekends. How is this sense of comfort false?

4. What does Alice's new diary symbolize?

5. Alice begins to talk to people in Southern California about why they ran away from home. She tries to find a common thread that makes kids want to leave their parents. Ultimately, she finds out that hair is something kids and parents argue about all the time. What does the argument over hair really mean?

Go Ask Alice Advanced Short Answer Unit Test Page 3

6. Describe the hallucination Alice had while on a bad acid trip and how the hallucination correlates with her injuries.

7. Does Alice get anything out of her group therapy? Explain your answer.

8. In the epilogue it says, "Was it an accidental overdose? A premeditated overdose? No one knows, and in some ways that question isn't important." What does the editor mean when she says that how Alice died isn't important? What is important to know about her death?

III. Vocabulary

Write down the vocabulary words given, then write a paragraph or two about *Go Ask Alice* correctly using all of the words.

IV. Essay

Analyze the role communication plays in Alice's life. Think about the different mediums of communication (writing, speaking, actions, etc) and the different people she communicates with throughout the novel (herself, parents, peers, therapists, etc). Highlight both positive and negative ways communication affects Alice's life and determine whether or not communication played a role in Alice's death.

MULTIPLE CHOICE UNIT TEST 1 - *Go Ask Alice*

I. Matching/Identify

____ 1. Tim
____ 2. Shrink
____ 3. New York
____ 4. Chris
____ 5. Jan
____ 6. Christmas
____ 7. Social Worker
____ 8. Alex
____ 9. Richie
____ 10. Denver
____ 11. Letter
____ 12. Grandpa
____ 13. Marcie
____ 14. Mountains
____ 15. Peanuts
____ 16. California
____ 17. New Year's
____ 18. Candy
____ 19. Fawn
____ 20. Babbie

A. Alice's favorite holiday
B. Person Alice envisions covered in maggots and worms
C. "Straight" girl who Alice is friends with
D. Person judge orders Alice to see
E. What Joel gives Alice while she is in the hospital
F. Alice thinks this is from Mr. Larsen
G. Location of mission that helps Alice
H. Boyfriend of Alice's that convinces her to start selling drugs
I. Place Alice's parents take her to avoid peer pressure at school
J. Shows up high while Alice is babysitting
K. Friend Alice makes at the mental hospital
L. How Alice thinks about giving her siblings drugs
M. Where Alice runs away the second time
N. Person Alice talks to about avoiding peer pressure and drugs
O. Opens a boutique with Alice near Berkeley
P. Alice's chosen career
Q. Alice's younger sister
R. Lies to judge about Alice selling drugs
S. Place Alice visits with her mom while her dad substitutes
T. When Alice bonds with family while cleaning in her pajamas

Go Ask Alice Multiple Choice Unit Test 1 Page 2

II. Multiple Choice

1. Describe the game "Button, Button, Who's Got the Button."
    - A. A tray of fourteen sodas is brought out. Ten of the drinks contain the drug LSD and the point is to figure out who got lucky with the drink laced with drugs.
    - B. Music plays as kids pass a button around the circle. When the music stops the person who has the button has to kiss the person who to his/her right.
    - C. LSD is put on the bottom of a button. The button is put in a basket with pennies. Each person takes one item from the basket and the person with the button gets high.
    - D. The numbers one through eight are placed in a basket. Someone draws a number and if there is a person wearing exactly that many buttons, they get to have the LSD.

2. Alice begins to sell drugs to help her boyfriend earn money. Who does she sell drugs to that makes her feel really guilty and upset?
    - A. Her sister's friends
    - B. Her little brother
    - C. Elementary school students
    - D. Homeless people

3. What happens to Alice and Chris that makes them leave San Francisco?
    - A. The two girls are high all the time and loose their jobs for not going to work. Because of this, they have no money to pay rent and are evicted from their apartment. They leave to make a fresh start somewhere new.
    - B. Alice gets a phone call from her parents. They girls are worried that since their parents know where they are that they will make them go home. They leave the city to hide from their parents once again.
    - C. Richie and some friends show up and threaten to kill Alice if she doesn't start selling drugs for him once again. The girls are terrified and flee the city that night.
    - D. The two girls are raped and sadistically brutalized by Shelia and her boyfriend while they are high one night. After being taken advantage of, they decide to leave.

4. How do other students react when Alice returns to school?
    - A. Several kids harass Alice and try to get her to sell them drugs like she used to. They don't believe she is clean.
    - B. Most of her friends are happy to see her. They go out of their way to provide extra support for her in keeping her away from people who use drugs.
    - C. Alice is a grade level behind so none of her old friends will talk to her. The younger kids have all heard rumors about her drug use and don't want to talk to her either.
    - D. Everyone ignores her. They are mad she left so suddenly and angry she never tried to call or contact them while gone.

Go Ask Alice Multiple Choice Unit Test 1 Page 3

5. When Alice runs away a second time, she continues writing but not in her diary. What does she use instead?
    A. Old newspapers from the park she sleeps in at night
    B. A new notebook she buys since she left her old diary at home
    C. A laptop she steals from an unsuspecting family on vacation
    D. Single sheets of paper, paper bags, and other items that happen to be around

6. How does Alice get money to buy drugs?
    A. She sells drugs for her dealer
    B. She works at a gas station four days a week
    C. She begs for money and performs sexual favors
    D. She steals from tourists

7. Why does Alice want to get a new diary when she gets back home?
    A. Alice feels like her first diary is her past, or her life on drugs. When she gets home she wants to start a new diary that will be her future, a life without drugs.
    B. Alice's old diary is already full. She needs a new one in order to have enough room to write all her thoughts.
    C. Alice lost her old diary when she ran away so she needs a new one to have a place to write her thoughts.
    D. Alice's old diary is falling apart from being used so often. She needs to start a new one so she doesn't lose pages from her old one.

8. What do the kids at school threaten to do to Alice's family?
    A. They threaten to severely beat up her siblings and burn down her family's home.
    B. They threaten to start dangerous rumors about her family to force them out of town.
    C. They threaten to give her younger siblings candy laced with drugs and plant drugs in her father's car so he will get fired.
    D. They threaten to hurt her fragile grandmother since she lives alone.

9. Describe the physical condition Alice is in at the hospital.
    A. Alice has third degree burns covering her arms and hands, her jaw is broken and wired shut so she can hardly speak, her ankle is broken, and she has blurry vision.
    B. Alice has a broken nose, her eyelids are bruised and swollen so that she can barely even see, she is missing a lot of hair, both her feet are broken, and she has to have four teeth replaced.
    C. Alice has two broken ribs, her leg is broken in two places, she has bruises all over her body, there are stitches covering most of her face, and she has a mild case of amnesia.
    D. Alice has torn off the tops of her fingers, she is missing fingernails, her face is scratched and clawed up, she is missing chunks of her hair and her scalp is exposed, her body is badly bruised, and several of her toes are broken.

Go Ask Alice Multiple Choice Unit Test 1 Page 4

10. What happens after Alice decides not to keep a diary?
    A. Nine months after Alice stops keeping a diary her and Joel have a baby and decide to get married.
    B. Five months after Alice stops keeping a diary she is back into drugs. She later finds out she has contracted AIDS from sharing needles with other users.
    C. Six weeks after Alice stops keeping a diary she runs away from home and is never heard from again.
    D. Three weeks after Alice stops keeping a diary she is found dead from an overdose on drugs.

III. Essay
Select *one* of the following topics and respond in an essay:

Alice begins to talk to people in Southern California about why they ran away from home. She tries to find a common thread that makes kids want to leave their parents. Ultimately, she finds out that hair is something kids and parents argue about all the time. What does the argument over hair really mean?

What did Alice's diary mean to her? Why was it important to her life?

Go Ask Alice Multiple Choice Unit Test 1 Page 5

IV. Vocabulary - Match the correct definitions to the words.

____ 1. Inferior A. Off or away from the correct path

____ 2. Gregarious B. Disagreement: point of disagreement

____ 3. Impregnable C. Common, boring, dull, unimaginative

____ 4. Echelon D. Unable to be captured, over thrown, or broken into

____ 5. Fink E. Something that is remarkable, impressive, or extraordinary

____ 6. Astray F. Distinct, fluent, meaningful, and clear in the power of speech

____ 7. Articulate G. Written statement or declaration made under oath

____ 8. Interminable H. Lower in position, rank, or worth

____ 9. Discreet I. Expressed grief or regret; mourned

____ 10. Affidavit J. Mental and emotional strength in facing difficulty

____ 11. Nonchalantly K. Cooly unconcerned; indifferent; casual

____ 12. Contention L. Edged or moved up sideways

____ 13. Mundane M. Level of command, authority, or rank

____ 14. Conscientious N. Showing wise self-restraint in behavior

____ 15. Conceive O. Seeking the company of others; outgoing and sociable

____ 16. Lamented P. Characterized by taking extreme care and/or making great effort

____ 17. Distinction Q. Informer, spy, or someone who squeals

____ 18. Fortitude R. Recognizing or distinguishing differences

____ 19. Sidled S. Unending

____ 20. Phenomena T. Imagine, form an idea

MULTIPLE CHOICE UNIT TEST 2 – *Go Ask Alice*

I. Matching/Identify

____ 1. Letter   A. Opens a boutique with Alice near Berkeley

____ 2. Peanuts   B. Alice's younger sister

____ 3. Marcie   C. Shows up high while Alice is babysitting

____ 4. Denver   D. Alice's favorite holiday

____ 5. Richie   E. Place Alice visits with her mom while her dad substitutes

____ 6. Babbie   F. How Alice thinks about giving her siblings drugs

____ 7. Christmas   G. "Straight" girl who Alice is friends with

____ 8. Fawn   H. Where Alice runs away the second time

____ 9. Mountains   I. Person Alice envisions covered in maggots and worms

____ 10. Candy   J. What Joel gives Alice while she is in the hospital

____ 11. Tim   K. When Alice bonds with family while cleaning in her pajamas

____ 12. Grandpa   L. Location of mission that helps Alice

____ 13. Alex   M. Boyfriend of Alice's that convinces her to start selling drugs

____ 14. New Year's   N. Alice thinks this is from Mr. Larsen

____ 15. Chris   O. Place Alice's parents take her to avoid peer pressure at school

____ 16. Jan   P. Lies to judge about Alice selling drugs

____ 17. Shrink   Q. Person Alice talks to about avoiding peer pressure and drugs

____ 18. Social Worker   R. Person judge orders Alice to see

____ 19. New York   S. Alice's chosen career

____ 20. California   T. Friend Alice makes at the mental hospital

Go Ask Alice Multiple Choice Unit Test 2 Page 2

II. Multiple Choice

1. Describe Alice's first high.
    A. Alice loses all her inhibitions and feels happy and carefree.
    B. Alice gets very sick and starts to throw up.
    C. Alice can't remember anything that happened that night.
    D. Alice was scared from the hallucinations and was hoping it would end soon.

2. According to Alice's friend, why do more kids prefer drugs to alcohol?
    A. Drugs give people a much better high than alcohol.
    B. Drugs are easier for teenagers to get than alcohol.
    C. Alcohol can be much more addictive than drugs.
    D. Alcohol is more expensive than drugs.

3. After vowing to never do drugs again, Alice and Chris get mixed up in the drug scene in San Francisco. What event prompts the two friends to begin using drugs again?
    A. Alice and Chris meet two boys they think are cute. They go on a double date and discover the boys have a stash of pot. They want the older boys to think they are mature, so they smoke with them.
    B. Chris's boss, Shelia, invites the girls to a party. When the girls get to the party they realize people are passing around joints and can't resist.
    C. Alice and Chris are both depressed about their life in San Francisco. Chris is able to get pot from a friend and the girls vow to use it just once to give them a little pick up.
    D. Mr. Mellani's son comes into the store one day worried his father might discover his drug habit. He gives Alice some joints to hold so that he won't get caught. Alice and Chris can't resist and figure since it was free they should smoke it.

4. Describe the new shop Alice and Chris open near Berkeley.
    A. They sell jewelry in a small shop near the college. They get a reputation in the town and begin to make even more money selling drugs to college kids.
    B. They open a shop that goes bankrupt soon after opening. They are forced to find new jobs to make money for the rent.
    C. They open a shop where college kids stop by to watch TV and sit around. There is a regular crowd and the business is fairly successful.
    D. They open a clothing shop that draws several wealthy women. The girls make so much money they open a part for children as well.

5. When Alice runs away a second time, she continues writing but not in her diary. What does she use instead?
    A. Old newspapers from the park she sleeps in at night
    B. A new notebook she buys since she left her old diary at home
    C. A laptop she steals from an unsuspecting family on vacation
    D. Single sheets of paper, paper bags, and other items that happen to be around

Go Ask Alice Multiple Choice Unit Test 2 Page 3

6. What do the people at the mission do for Alice?
    A. Let her take a shower, give her clothes, feed her, take her to the doctor
    B. Give her a safe place to sleep and money for food
    C. Take her to the doctor and call her parents to come get her immediately
    D. Give her a job cleaning and cooking food for some extra money

7. Alice is worried that with all the sex she is having she may get pregnant. Why can't she take the birth control pill to protect herself?
    A. Alice knows that she has to be 18 in order to get the pill. Since it is too hard to get illegally and she is not yet an adult, she can't take it.
    B. Alice uses so many drugs and blacks out so often that she can rarely tell what day it is. She can't take the pill for protection unless she can remember to take it each day, so she just hopes she doesn't end up pregnant.
    C. Alice tries taking the pill and realizes that it takes away from her high. She doesn't want to lose her great highs, so she won't take it.
    D. Alice's doctor warns her that the pill will react badly with the drugs she uses. She could die from the combination of the two drugs, so she can't take it.

8. How does Alice perform as a student when she returns to school?
    A. She struggles to make up all the work she missed. She makes several low grades since she is so far behind.
    B. She continues as an average student making average grades just like she did before she left.
    C. She becomes a devoted student who studies several hours each night. She makes high grades in all her classes.
    D. She does really well in her elective classes, but still has a hard time with her grades in clsses like math and English.

9. How does Alice meet Joel?
    A. Alice begins taking piano lessons once again. Her teacher was sick one day and referred her to Joel for a substitute lesson.
    B. Alice volunteers in her sister's elementary school as part of her agreement with the court. She meets Joel also volunteering at the school.
    C. Alice and her mother are out picking up a prescription for her grandmother. She meets Joel when he helps them in the pharmacy.
    D. Alice's dad gets special permission for her to use the university library. While she is there studying one afternoon she meets Joel.

Go Ask Alice Multiple Choice Unit Test 2 Page 4

10. Describe the physical condition Alice is in at the hospital.
    A. Alice has third degree burns covering her arms and hands, her jaw is broken and wired shut so she can hardly speak, her ankle is broken, and she has blurry vision.
    B. Alice has a broken nose, her eyelids are bruised and swollen so that she can barely even see, she is missing a lot of hair, both her feet are broken, and she has to have four teeth replaced.
    C. Alice has two broken ribs, her leg is broken in two places, she has bruises all over her body, there are stitches covering most of her face, and she has a mild case of amnesia.
    D. Alice has torn off the tops of her fingers, she is missing fingernails, her face is scratched and clawed up, she is missing chunks of her hair and her scalp is exposed, her body is badly bruised, and several of her toes are broken.

III. Essay
Select *one* of the following topics and respond in an essay:

Alice commits to not doing drugs several times throughout the novel. Despite how hard she tries, she still falls back to using drugs. Do you think the situations she puts herself in and the people she associates with influence her use of drugs? Use details from the text to support your answer.

In the epilogue it says, "Was it an accidental overdose? A premeditated overdose? No one knows, and in some ways that question isn't important." What does the editor mean when she says that how Alice died isn't important? What is important to know about her death?

Go Ask Alice Multiple Choice Unit Test 2 Page 5

IV. Vocabulary - Match the correct definitions to the words.

____ 1. Stifling   A. Off or away from the correct path

____ 2. Teeming   B. Disagreement; point of disagreement

____ 3. Discreet   C. Revengeful with the desire to hurt another

____ 4. Blase   D. Unable to be captured, overthrown, or broken into

____ 5. Articulate   E. Pursuing with harassment; annoy persistently

____ 6. Firmament   F. Distinct, fluent, meaningful, and clear in the power of speech

____ 7. Conscientious   G. Assault; attack

____ 8. Siege   H. Lower in position, rank, or worth

____ 9. Impregnable   I. The feeling that someone or something is unworthy of one's consideration or respect

____ 10. Entity   J. Mental and emotional strength in facing difficulty

____ 11. Vindictive   K. Accusations in response to accusations from someone else

____ 12. Fortitude   L. Bored with life or unimpressed

____ 13. Vacillating   M. Smothering or suffocating

____ 14. Disdain   N. Showing wise self-restraint in behavior

____ 15. Recrimination   O. Full of things; swarming with

____ 16. Inferior   P. Characterized by taking extreme care and/or making great effort

____ 17. Persecuting   Q. The expanse of the sky

____ 18. Astray   R. To have complete possession of; to dominate

____ 19. Monopolize   S. Something that exists as its own self or being

____ 20. Contention   T. Indecisive; unsteady; wavering

ANSWER SHEET - *Go Ask Alice*
Multiple Choice Unit Test 1

I. Matching	II. Multiple Choice	IV. Vocabulary
1. N	1. A	1. H
2. D	2. C	2. O
3. S	3. D	3. D
4. O	4. A	4. M
5. J	5. D	5. Q
6. A	6. C	6. A
7. P	7. A	7. F
8. Q	8. C	8. S
9. H	9. D	9. N
10. M	10. D	10. G
11. E		11. K
12. B		12. B
13. R		13. C
14. I		14. P
15. F		15. T
16. G		16. I
17. T		17. R
18. L		18. J
19. C		19. L
20. K		20. E

ANSWER SHEET - *Go Ask Alice*
Multiple Choice Unit Test 2

I. Matching	II. Multiple Choice	IV. Vocabulary
1. J	1. A	1. M
2. N	2. B	2. O
3. P	3. B	3. N
4. H	4. C	4. L
5. M	5. D	5. F
6. T	6. A	6. Q
7. D	7. B	7. P
8. G	8. C	8. G
9. O	9. D	9. D
10. F	10. D	10. S
11. Q		11. C
12. I		12. J
13. B		13. T
14. K		14. I
15. A		15. K
16. C		16. H
17. R		17. E
18. S		18. A
19. E		19. R
20. L		20. B

UNIT RESOURCE MATERIALS

BULLETIN BOARD IDEAS - *Go Ask Alice*

1. Save one corner of the board for the best of students' *Go Ask Alice* writing assignments.

2. Take one of the word search puzzles from the extra activities packet and with a marker copy it over in a large size on the bulletin board. Write the clue words to find to one side. Invite students prior to and after class to find the words and circle them on the bulletin board.

3. Write several of the most significant quotations from the book onto the board on brightly colored paper.

4. Make a bulletin board listing the vocabulary words for this unit. As you complete sections of the novel and discuss the vocabulary for each section, write the definitions on the bulletin board. (If your board is one students face frequently, it will help them learn the words.)

5. Post photos and information about people who have overcome a battle with drugs. Many teenage magazines run feature stories on teenagers who have been addicted to drugs and students would most likely enjoy articles from magazines they like to read.

6. Create a bulletin board with a communication theme. Place facts, information, and tips for better communication between teens and parents. You may also want to have information about peer pressure and communication with other teens.

7. Create a bulletin board about censorship. Post lists of the most frequently banned books in the United States and use quotations about censorship to encourage your students to think about where they stand on the issue.

8. Make a bulletin board covering other teen issues. You could post facts/statistics on drinking, drugs, dropping out, pregnancy, rape, etc. Next to each group of statistics, print out colorful copies of young adult novel covers that deal with those issues. A list of suggested novels and the topics they cover is listed below.
    - Drugs: *Crank* by Ellen Hopkins, *Impulse* by Ellen Hopkins
    - Cutting: *Cut* by Patricia McCormick
    - Eating Disorders: *Diary of an Anorexic Girl* by Morgan Menzie
    - Teen Pregnancy: *Make Lemonade* by Virginia Euwer Wolff, *Catalyst* by Laurie Halse Anderson
    - Dropping Out: *Make Lemonade* by Virginia Euwer Wolff
    - Suicide: *Burn Journals* by Brent Runyon, *Impulse* by Ellen Hopkins
    - Violence against others: *Burned* by Ellen Hopkins
    - Rape: *Lovely Bones* by Alice Sebold, *Speak* by Laurie Halse Anderson

9. Make a bulletin board with colorful copies of other diaries Dr. Beatrice Sparks has edited. Write a short tease for the book to get students interested.

EXTRA ACTIVITIES – Go Ask Alice

One of the difficulties in teaching a novel is that all students don't read at the same speed. One student who likes to read may take the book home and finish it in a day or two. Sometimes a few students finish the in-class assignments early. The problem, then, is finding suitable extra activities for students.

One thing that seems to help is to keep a little library in the classroom. For this unit on *Go Ask Alice*, you might check out from the school library other diaries edited by Dr. Beatrice Sparks. The novels listed in the bulletin board section that cover other teen issues would also be good titles to have in your room as well.

Other things you may keep on hand are puzzles. We have made some relating directly to *Go Ask Alice* for you. Feel free to duplicate them for your students to use.

Some students may like to draw. You might devise a contest or allow some extra-credit grade for students who draw characters or scenes from *Go Ask Alice*. Note, too, that if the students do not want to keep their drawings you may pick up some extra bulletin board materials this way. If you have a contest and you supply the prize (a CD or something like that perhaps), you could, possibly, make the drawing itself a non-returnable entry fee.

The pages which follow contain games, puzzles and worksheets. The keys, when appropriate, immediately follow the puzzle or worksheet. There are two main groups of activities: one group for the unit; that is, generally relating to *Go Ask Alice* text, and another group of activities related strictly to *Go Ask Alice* vocabulary.

Directions for these games, puzzles and worksheets are self-explanatory. The object here is to provide you with extra materials you may use in any way you choose.

MORE ACTIVITIES - *Go Ask Alice*

1. Have students design a new book cover (front and back and inside flaps) for *Go Ask Alice*.

2. Have students select a character from the book and complete the "I Am" poem from that character's point of view. (see the following handout)

3. Have students group the chapters together to show the larger structure of the novel. Have them explain why they chose the divisions they made.

4. Have students choose one chapter of the book (with sufficient action) to rewrite as a play. In conjunction with this assignment, have students write a composition explaining the difficulties they encountered in changing from one written form to another.

5. Have students write out the characters in the book and cast famous actors and actress for an updated movie version of the novel. Instruct students to write a brief explanation as to why the actor/actress they selected would be perfect for the part.

6. Have students create a soundtrack for *Go Ask Alice*. Have students burn a cd of the songs, design a cd cover, and include a brief explanation as to why they selected each song.

7. Have students further explore the validity of the diary. Instruct students to use the internet to find articles and information to determine whether or not the diary is real.

8. Since Alice's diary is meant to help others, have students write a short story about an experience from their life that can help others learn from a past mistake.

9. Have students write an ending to the diary. Instruct them to pick up at the last date and continue adding entries for the three weeks that lead to her death.

10. Have students write a letter to their parents. In this letter, ask them to analyze the way they communicate now, and offer suggestions for improvements.

11. Have students conduct additional research on censorship. Prompt them to read a commonly banned book and determine whether or not the ban is appropriate.

12. Have students write a letter to the editor of the book (see the following handout). Letters can be mailed to:
    Dr. Beatrice Sparks
    c/o Simon & Schuster Publicity Department
    Simon & Schuster, Inc.
    1230 Avenue of the Americas
    New York, NY 10020

Letter to the Editor

Often times, books are written to make people think about serious issues. Think about the point the editor was trying to make in putting together this diary. Then, compose a letter to the editor expressing how this book has affected your life.

Topics to include in your letter:
- What you liked about the book
- How you could relate to this book
- How realistic the book was
- What you learned from the book
- What issues the book made you think about
- How you felt when reading the book
- How you have changed since reading the book
- Anything else you think the editor should know

Necessary Elements:
- Your letter must by typed
- You should begin your letter by saying Dear Mr. (or Ms.) _____,
- You should have an introductory paragraph where you introduce yourself
- You should have body paragraphs
- You should have a friendly conclusion to the letter
- Underneath your signature you should include your home address and email address in case the editor wishes to write you back

Remember to proofread this letter and turn it in to me free of errors. I will grade your letter, allow you to make any changes that are needed, and then I will mail your letters to the editor of the diary. Most editors enjoy receiving letters from readers and like to see how their hard work has affected others. Some may even respond to letters from their readers, so don't be surprised if you get a reply.

"I Am" Poem

Complete this "I am" poem. You may select any character from the book to do this poem about. Be sure to write from his or her point of view and think about the things he or she would feel. You may use some short one word answers, but do not make each line only a few words. You should try to provide support from the novel to really develop this poem so that it reveals information and insight about the character you select.

I am (2 characteristics your character has)
I wonder (something your character wonders)
I hear (something real or imaginary your character hears)
I see (something real or imaginary your character sees)
I want (something your character desires)
I am (the first line of the poem repeated)

I pretend (something your character pretends to do)
I feel (something real or imaginary your character feels emotionally)
I touch (something real or imaginary your character would touch physically)
I worry (something your characters worries about)
I cry (something that makes your character upset)
I am (the first line of the poem repeated)

I understand (something your character knows)
I say (something your character believes in)
I dream (something your character would dream about)
I try (something your character makes an effort to do)
I hope (something your character hopes for)
I am (the first line of the poem repeated)

Go Ask Alice Word List

No.	Word	Clue/Definition
1.	ALEX	Alice's younger sister
2.	ALICE	She wrote the diary and died.
3.	BABBIE	Girl in mental hospital whose parents decide to give her up to foster care
4.	BOUTIQUE	Kind of store Alice and Chris open
5.	CANDY	What Alice wants to put drugs on to get her younger brother to experience being high
6.	CAR	Kids at school threaten to hide drugs in Alice's father's ___ to get him in trouble.
7.	CHICAGO	City where Joel lives
8.	CHRIS	Girl Alice runs away with
9.	CHRISTMAS	Alice's favorite holiday
10.	CLEANING	Alice has fun doing this with her family after a New Year's Eve party.
11.	DENVER	City Alice first goes to the second time she runs away
12.	DIARY	What Alice locks in a metal box
13.	DINNER	Alice makes this for her mother as a surprise for her birthday.
14.	ELEMENTARY	Alice is ashamed that she sells drugs at the ___ school.
15.	FAWN	'Straight' girl Alice becomes friends with
16.	GRANDMA	Alice stays to help her around the house over the summer.
17.	GRANDPA	He has a heart attack and dies.
18.	HAPPINESS	Kitten belonging to Alice's sister; makes Alice appreciate the pleasures of life without drugs
19.	JAN	Girl who shows up high while Alice is babysitting
20.	JEWELRY	While in San Francisco, Alice works at a shop that sells this.
21.	JILL	Girl's house where Alice played 'Button, Button, Who's Got the Button?'
22.	JOEL	Boy Alice meets at the university library; he is supportive
23.	LARSEN	Last name of the family Alice babysits for
24.	LETTER	Joel sends Alice this while she is in the hospital.
25.	LSD	Drug in Alice's Coke when she first took drugs
26.	MARCIE	Girl who lies to the judge and gets Alice sent to a mental hospital
27.	MISSION	People who take Alice to the doctor & give her food & clothes
28.	MOUNTAINS	Place Alice's parents take Chris and Alice for a fun weekend away from the kids at school
29.	PEANUTS	They were covered in acid, sending Alice on a bad trip ending with her going to the hospital.
30.	PIANO	Instrument Alice plays
31.	PREGNANT	Because Alice is worried she is ___, she can't sleep, and the doctor prescribes tranquilizers.
32.	PROFESSOR	The job of Alice's father
33.	RICHIE	Name of boyfriend who got Alice into selling drugs
34.	ROGER	Boy Alice really likes; he stands her up at the start of the book
35.	SHELIA	Chris's employer; turns the girls onto drugs in San Francisco
36.	TIM	Alice's younger brother

Word Search - Go Ask Alice

```
L R D S R E T T E L M O U N T A I N S Z
A C I R O G Q Y S Y V G V Q B I M G Q G
R D A P G R B T P R Z A C J Z A M R C F
S J R P E A U R P A Q C R W S K B Y P Q
E T Y K R N S A M T S I R H C G R B K J
N Z M B A D Q B L N R H X J M L N J I T
K H G E W M B W S E O C Y K E K M V D E
P Y P L P A D V F M S C T W M P H T H B
S R G R A N D P A E S N E M Z B D F Y P
K H E R G W T F H L E J P A H F I D J K
R Q D G G J F P G E F F C R J H N B K M
C G S W N X A N P H O C G C T A N H K Y
L N X X V A W O S G R J L I C Q E L X Y
D E N V E R N H A P P I N E S S R D S V
R E Q N J A F T N B N K U Y A A Y Q G D
Y C K O I R A N D J O Q T B C N R D X B
R I E P Z I X M Y S I T Q J T I I X H L
A L E X L L I J G T S I R H C J A N Q R
J A N E N C Y K U V S J Y H V R S H G D
K R H F R V Y O Z S I V I R Z W D R X X
C S S P H G B Q Y D M E X F N Y P B J T
```

ALEX	CHRISTMAS	GRANDPA	LSD	RICHIE
ALICE	CLEANING	HAPPINESS	MARCIE	ROGER
BABBIE	DENVER	JAN	MISSION	SHELIA
BOUTIQUE	DIARY	JEWELRY	MOUNTAINS	TIM
CANDY	DINNER	JILL	PEANUTS	
CAR	ELEMENTARY	JOEL	PIANO	
CHICAGO	FAWN	LARSEN	PREGNANT	
CHRIS	GRANDMA	LETTER	PROFESSOR	

Word Search Answer Key - Go Ask Alice

ALEX	CHRISTMAS	GRANDPA	LSD	RICHIE
ALICE	CLEANING	HAPPINESS	MARCIE	ROGER
BABBIE	DENVER	JAN	MISSION	SHELIA
BOUTIQUE	DIARY	JEWELRY	MOUNTAINS	TIM
CANDY	DINNER	JILL	PEANUTS	
CAR	ELEMENTARY	JOEL	PIANO	
CHICAGO	FAWN	LARSEN	PREGNANT	
CHRIS	GRANDMA	LETTER	PROFESSOR	

Crossword - Go Ask Alice

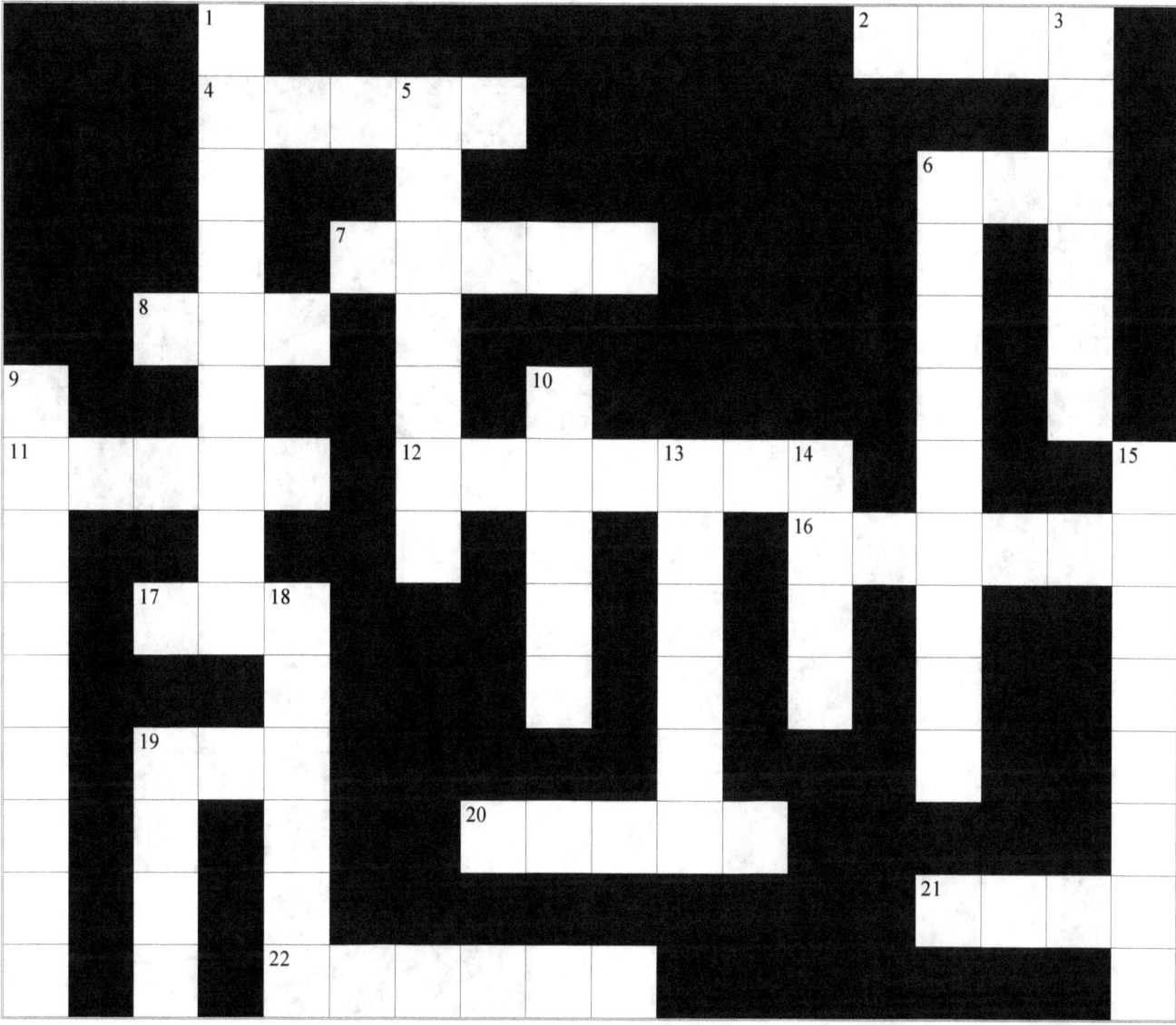

Across

2. Girl's house where Alice played 'Button, Button, Who's Got the Button?'
4. She wrote the diary and died.
6. Kids at school threaten to hide drugs in Alice's father's ___ to get him in trouble.
7. Instrument Alice plays
8. Alice's younger brother
11. Boy Alice really likes; he stands her up at the start of the book
12. Alice stays to help her around the house over the summer.
16. Joel sends Alice this while she is in the hospital.
17. Drug in Alice's Coke when she first took drugs
19. Girl who shows up high while Alice is babysitting
20. What Alice locks in a metal box
21. 'Straight' girl Alice becomes friends with
22. Name of boyfriend who got Alice into selling drugs

Down

1. Kitten belonging to Alice's sister; makes Alice appreciate the pleasures of life without drugs
3. Last name of the family Alice babysits for
5. City where Joel lives
6. Alice's favorite holiday
9. The job of Alice's father
10. What Alice wants to put drugs on to get her younger brother to experience being high
13. City Alice first goes to the second time she runs away
14. Alice's younger sister
15. Because Alice is worried she is ___, she can't sleep, and the doctor prescribes tranquilizers.
18. Alice makes this for her mother as a surprise for her birthday.
19. Boy Alice meets at the university library; he is supportive

Crossword Answer Key - Go Ask Alice

Across
2. Girl's house where Alice played 'Button, Button, Who's Got the Button?'
4. She wrote the diary and died.
6. Kids at school threaten to hide drugs in Alice's father's ___ to get him in trouble.
7. Instrument Alice plays
8. Alice's younger brother
11. Boy Alice really likes; he stands her up at the start of the book
12. Alice stays to help her around the house over the summer.
16. Joel sends Alice this while she is in the hospital.
17. Drug in Alice's Coke when she first took drugs
19. Girl who shows up high while Alice is babysitting
20. What Alice locks in a metal box
21. 'Straight' girl Alice becomes friends with
22. Name of boyfriend who got Alice into selling drugs

Down
1. Kitten belonging to Alice's sister; makes Alice appreciate the pleasures of life without drugs
3. Last name of the family Alice babysits for
5. City where Joel lives
6. Alice's favorite holiday
9. The job of Alice's father
10. What Alice wants to put drugs on to get her younger brother to experience being high
13. City Alice first goes to the second time she runs away
14. Alice's younger sister
15. Because Alice is worried she is ___, she can't sleep, and the doctor prescribes tranquilizers.
18. Alice makes this for her mother as a surprise for her birthday.
19. Boy Alice meets at the university library; he is supportive

Matching 1 - Go Ask Alice

___ 1. JILL   A. Instrument Alice plays

___ 2. ALICE   B. Girl Alice runs away with

___ 3. CAR   C. While in San Francisco, Alice works at a shop that sells this.

___ 4. GRANDMA   D. Alice's younger brother

___ 5. LETTER   E. Alice's younger sister

___ 6. CHRISTMAS   F. Kitten belonging to Alice's sister; makes Alice appreciate the pleasures of life without drugs

___ 7. SHELIA   G. Boy Alice really likes; he stands her up at the start of the book

___ 8. RICHIE   H. Chris's employer; turns the girls onto drugs in San Francisco

___ 9. CHRIS   I. What Alice wants to put drugs on to get her younger brother to experience being high

___ 10. DINNER   J. Drug in Alice's Coke when she first took drugs

___ 11. LSD   K. Name of boyfriend who got Alice into selling drugs

___ 12. PROFESSOR   L. Last name of the family Alice babysits for

___ 13. GRANDPA   M. He has a heart attack and dies.

___ 14. LARSEN   N. Kids at school threaten to hide drugs in Alice's father's ___ to get him in trouble.

___ 15. MARCIE   O. She wrote the diary and died.

___ 16. ALEX   P. The job of Alice's father

___ 17. JEWELRY   Q. Girl who lies to the judge and gets Alice sent to a mental hospital

___ 18. JOEL   R. Boy Alice meets at the university library; he is supportive

___ 19. CANDY   S. Place Alice's parents take Chris and Alice for a fun weekend away from the kids at school

___ 20. ROGER   T. Alice's favorite holiday

___ 21. MOUNTAINS   U. Girl's house where Alice played 'Button, Button, Who's Got the Button?'

___ 22. PIANO   V. Alice stays to help her around the house over the summer.

___ 23. TIM   W. Joel sends Alice this while she is in the hospital.

___ 24. DIARY   X. Alice makes this for her mother as a surprise for her birthday.

___ 25. HAPPINESS   Y. What Alice locks in a metal box

Matching 1 Answer Key - Go Ask Alice

U - 1. JILL		A. Instrument Alice plays
O - 2. ALICE		B. Girl Alice runs away with
N - 3. CAR		C. While in San Francisco, Alice works at a shop that sells this.
V - 4. GRANDMA		D. Alice's younger brother
W - 5. LETTER		E. Alice's younger sister
T - 6. CHRISTMAS		F. Kitten belonging to Alice's sister; makes Alice appreciate the pleasures of life without drugs
H - 7. SHELIA		G. Boy Alice really likes; he stands her up at the start of the book
K - 8. RICHIE		H. Chris's employer; turns the girls onto drugs in San Francisco
B - 9. CHRIS		I. What Alice wants to put drugs on to get her younger brother to experience being high
X - 10. DINNER		J. Drug in Alice's Coke when she first took drugs
J - 11. LSD		K. Name of boyfriend who got Alice into selling drugs
P - 12. PROFESSOR		L. Last name of the family Alice babysits for
M - 13. GRANDPA		M. He has a heart attack and dies.
L - 14. LARSEN		N. Kids at school threaten to hide drugs in Alice's father's ___ to get him in trouble.
Q - 15. MARCIE		O. She wrote the diary and died.
E - 16. ALEX		P. The job of Alice's father
C - 17. JEWELRY		Q. Girl who lies to the judge and gets Alice sent to a mental hospital
R - 18. JOEL		R. Boy Alice meets at the university library; he is supportive
I - 19. CANDY		S. Place Alice's parents take Chris and Alice for a fun weekend away from the kids at school
G - 20. ROGER		T. Alice's favorite holiday
S - 21. MOUNTAINS		U. Girl's house where Alice played 'Button, Button, Who's Got the Button?'
A - 22. PIANO		V. Alice stays to help her around the house over the summer.
D - 23. TIM		W. Joel sends Alice this while she is in the hospital.
Y - 24. DIARY		X. Alice makes this for her mother as a surprise for her birthday.
F - 25. HAPPINESS		Y. What Alice locks in a metal box

Matching 2 - Go Ask Alice

___ 1. PROFESSOR   A. Alice makes this for her mother as a surprise for her birthday.

___ 2. GRANDMA   B. Girl in mental hospital whose parents decide to give her up to foster care

___ 3. MISSION   C. Chris's employer; turns the girls onto drugs in San Francisco

___ 4. DIARY   D. Because Alice is worried she is ___, she can't sleep, and the doctor prescribes tranquilizers.

___ 5. CLEANING   E. Boy Alice really likes; he stands her up at the start of the book

___ 6. PIANO   F. Alice's younger brother

___ 7. JAN   G. Alice's favorite holiday

___ 8. DENVER   H. City Alice first goes to the second time she runs away

___ 9. RICHIE   I. Alice stays to help her around the house over the summer.

___ 10. GRANDPA   J. Instrument Alice plays

___ 11. CHICAGO   K. Alice has fun doing this with her family after a New Year's Eve party.

___ 12. JOEL   L. Girl's house where Alice played 'Button, Button, Who's Got the Button?'

___ 13. TIM   M. Boy Alice meets at the university library; he is supportive

___ 14. SHELIA   N. City where Joel lives

___ 15. ROGER   O. What Alice locks in a metal box

___ 16. DINNER   P. Girl Alice runs away with

___ 17. BABBIE   Q. People who take Alice to the doctor & give her food & clothes

___ 18. JILL   R. 'Straight' girl Alice becomes friends with

___ 19. LETTER   S. Alice is ashamed that she sells drugs at the ___ school.

___ 20. CHRISTMAS   T. Name of boyfriend who got Alice into selling drugs

___ 21. FAWN   U. Kitten belonging to Alice's sister; makes Alice appreciate the pleasures of life without drugs

___ 22. ELEMENTARY   V. He has a heart attack and dies.

___ 23. HAPPINESS   W. Girl who shows up high while Alice is babysitting

___ 24. PREGNANT   X. The job of Alice's father

___ 25. CHRIS   Y. Joel sends Alice this while she is in the hospital.

Answer Key Matching 2 - Go Ask Alice

X - 1. PROFESSOR	A. Alice makes this for her mother as a surprise for her birthday.
I - 2. GRANDMA	B. Girl in mental hospital whose parents decide to give her up to foster care
Q - 3. MISSION	C. Chris's employer; turns the girls onto drugs in San Francisco
O - 4. DIARY	D. Because Alice is worried she is ___, she can't sleep, and the doctor prescribes tranquilizers.
K - 5. CLEANING	E. Boy Alice really likes; he stands her up at the start of the book
J - 6. PIANO	F. Alice's younger brother
W - 7. JAN	G. Alice's favorite holiday
H - 8. DENVER	H. City Alice first goes to the second time she runs away
T - 9. RICHIE	I. Alice stays to help her around the house over the summer.
V - 10. GRANDPA	J. Instrument Alice plays
N - 11. CHICAGO	K. Alice has fun doing this with her family after a New Year's Eve party.
M - 12. JOEL	L. Girl's house where Alice played 'Button, Button, Who's Got the Button?'
F - 13. TIM	M. Boy Alice meets at the university library; he is supportive
C - 14. SHELIA	N. City where Joel lives
E - 15. ROGER	O. What Alice locks in a metal box
A - 16. DINNER	P. Girl Alice runs away with
B - 17. BABBIE	Q. People who take Alice to the doctor & give her food & clothes
L - 18. JILL	R. 'Straight' girl Alice becomes friends with
Y - 19. LETTER	S. Alice is ashamed that she sells drugs at the ___ school.
G - 20. CHRISTMAS	T. Name of boyfriend who got Alice into selling drugs
R - 21. FAWN	U. Kitten belonging to Alice's sister; makes Alice appreciate the pleasures of life without drugs
S - 22. ELEMENTARY	V. He has a heart attack and dies.
U - 23. HAPPINESS	W. Girl who shows up high while Alice is babysitting
D - 24. PREGNANT	X. The job of Alice's father
P - 25. CHRIS	Y. Joel sends Alice this while she is in the hospital.

Juggle Letters 1 - Go Ask Alice

1. OGRER = 1. _____
   Boy Alice really likes; he stands her up at the start of the book

2. SIHRC = 2. _____
   Girl Alice runs away with

3. ITM = 3. _____
   Alice's younger brother

4. AUTPESN = 4. _____
   They were covered in acid, sending Alice on a bad trip ending with her going to the hospital.

5. ABIBBE = 5. _____
   Girl in mental hospital whose parents decide to give her up to foster care

6. AJN = 6. _____
   Girl who shows up high while Alice is babysitting

7. MNADGAR = 7. _____
   Alice stays to help her around the house over the summer.

8. YDAIR = 8. _____
   What Alice locks in a metal box

9. HCGIAOC = 9. _____
   City where Joel lives

10. WJLEREY =10. _____
    While in San Francisco, Alice works at a shop that sells this.

11. AELCI =11. _____
    She wrote the diary and died.

12. EJOL =12. _____
    Boy Alice meets at the university library; he is supportive

13. NNETGRAP =13. _____
    Because Alice is worried she is ___, she can't sleep, and the doctor prescribes tranquilizers.

14. ERIDNN =14. _____
    Alice makes this for her mother as a surprise for her birthday.

15. SRTISHCAM =15. _____
    Alice's favorite holiday

Answer Key Juggle Letters 1 - Go Ask Alice

1. OGRER = 1. ROGER

   Boy Alice really likes; he stands her up at the start of the book

2. SIHRC = 2. CHRIS

   Girl Alice runs away with

3. ITM = 3. TIM

   Alice's younger brother

4. AUTPESN = 4. PEANUTS

   They were covered in acid, sending Alice on a bad trip ending with her going to the hospital.

5. ABIBBE = 5. BABBIE

   Girl in mental hospital whose parents decide to give her up to foster care

6. AJN = 6. JAN

   Girl who shows up high while Alice is babysitting

7. MNADGAR = 7. GRANDMA

   Alice stays to help her around the house over the summer.

8. YDAIR = 8. DIARY

   What Alice locks in a metal box

9. HCGIAOC = 9. CHICAGO

   City where Joel lives

10. WJLEREY = 10. JEWELRY

    While in San Francisco, Alice works at a shop that sells this.

11. AELCI = 11. ALICE

    She wrote the diary and died.

12. EJOL = 12. JOEL

    Boy Alice meets at the university library; he is supportive

13. NNETGRAP = 13. PREGNANT

    Because Alice is worried she is ___, she can't sleep, and the doctor prescribes tranquilizers.

14. ERIDNN = 14. DINNER

    Alice makes this for her mother as a surprise for her birthday.

15. SRTISHCAM = 15. CHRISTMAS

    Alice's favorite holiday

Juggle Letters 2 - Go Ask Alice

1. RAIDY = 1. _____
   What Alice locks in a metal box

2. WERLJYE = 2. _____
   While in San Francisco, Alice works at a shop that sells this.

3. YTRENLEAEM = 3. _____
   Alice is ashamed that she sells drugs at the ___ school.

4. ENSARL = 4. _____
   Last name of the family Alice babysits for

5. DSL = 5. _____
   Drug in Alice's Coke when she first took drugs

6. EOUUQTIB = 6. _____
   Kind of store Alice and Chris open

7. UINSNOTMA = 7. _____
   Place Alice's parents take Chris and Alice for a fun weekend away from the kids at school

8. NCAYD = 8. _____
   What Alice wants to put drugs on to get her younger brother to experience being high

9. TSRICASHM = 9. _____
   Alice's favorite holiday

10. NNGICLAE =10. _____
    Alice has fun doing this with her family after a New Year's Eve party.

11. NISSMOI =11. _____
    People who take Alice to the doctor & give her food & clothes

12. HIRCIE =12. _____
    Name of boyfriend who got Alice into selling drugs

13. VENERD =13. _____
    City Alice first goes to the second time she runs away

14. ALSIHE =14. _____
    Chris's employer; turns the girls onto drugs in San Francisco

15. LIECA =15. _____
    She wrote the diary and died.

Answer Key Juggle Letters 2 - Go Ask Alice

1. RAIDY = 1. DIARY
What Alice locks in a metal box

2. WERLJYE = 2. JEWELRY
While in San Francisco, Alice works at a shop that sells this.

3. YTRENLEAEM = 3. ELEMENTARY
Alice is ashamed that she sells drugs at the ___ school.

4. ENSARL = 4. LARSEN
Last name of the family Alice babysits for

5. DSL = 5. LSD
Drug in Alice's Coke when she first took drugs

6. EOUUQTIB = 6. BOUTIQUE
Kind of store Alice and Chris open

7. UINSNOTMA = 7. MOUNTAINS
Place Alice's parents take Chris and Alice for a fun weekend away from the kids at school

8. NCAYD = 8. CANDY
What Alice wants to put drugs on to get her younger brother to experience being high

9. TSRICASHM = 9. CHRISTMAS
Alice's favorite holiday

10. NNGICLAE = 10. CLEANING
Alice has fun doing this with her family after a New Year's Eve party.

11. NISSMOI = 11. MISSION
People who take Alice to the doctor & give her food & clothes

12. HIRCIE = 12. RICHIE
Name of boyfriend who got Alice into selling drugs

13. VENERD = 13. DENVER
City Alice first goes to the second time she runs away

14. ALSIHE = 14. SHELIA
Chris's employer; turns the girls onto drugs in San Francisco

15. LIECA = 15. ALICE
She wrote the diary and died.

VOCABULARY RESOURCE MATERIALS

Go Ask Alice Vocabulary Word List

No.	Word	Clue/Definition
1.	AFFIDAVIT	Written statement or declaration made under oath
2.	ASTRAY	Off or away from the correct or right path
3.	CONCEIVE	Imagine; form an idea of
4.	DISCREET	Showing wise self-restraint in behavior
5.	ECHELON	Level of command, authority, or rank
6.	FOREBODING	Strong feeling of coming misfortune or evil
7.	INFERIOR	Lower in position, rank, or worth
8.	LECHEROUS	Suggestive; lustful
9.	NONCHALANTLY	In a way cooly unconcerned, indifferent, or casual
10.	PHENOMENA	Something that is remarkable, impressive, or extraordinary
11.	RAVINGS	Wild, delirious, or frenzied talking
12.	SIEGE	Assault; attack
13.	VACILLATING	Indecisive; unsteady; wavering
14.	ANTAGONISTIC	Hostile; unfriendly
15.	BLASE	Bored with life or unimpressed
16.	CONSCIENTIOUS	Characterized by taking extreme care and/or making great effort
17.	DISDAIN	The feeling that someone or something is unworthy of one's consideration or respect
18.	ENTITY	Something that exists as its own self or being
19.	FORTITUDE	Mental and emotional strength in facing difficulty
20.	INSCRIPTION	Marking of words or a message on an item
21.	MONOPOLIZE	To have complete possession of; to dominate
22.	PENANCE	Act of devotion to pay for a sin or wrongdoing
23.	PREMONITIONS	Advance warnings of the future
24.	RECRIMINATIONS	Accusations in response to accusations from someone else
25.	STIFLING	Smothering or suffocating
26.	VINDICTIVE	Revengeful; with the desire to hurt another
27.	ARTICULATE	Distinct, fluent, meaningful, and clear in the power of speech
28.	BLEARY	Blurred from sleep or fatigue; unclear
29.	CONTENTION	Disagreement; point of disagreement
30.	DISSERTATION	Lengthy, formal speech or writing about a particular topic
31.	FINK	Informer, spy, or someone who squeals
32.	GREGARIOUS	Seeking the company of others; outgoing and sociable
33.	INTERMINABLE	Unending
34.	MUNDANE	Common; dull; boring; unimaginative
35.	PERCEPTIVE	Understanding with insight or intuition
36.	PRODIGAL	Wastefully extravagant
37.	REVELATION	Something that is uncovered, not previously known
38.	TEEMING	Full of things; swarming
39.	ASININE	Foolish; silly; stupid
40.	CLODDY	Stupid or of lesser dignity or value
41.	DEGENERATE	One who falls below the desirable level of quality
42.	DISTINCTION	Recognizing or distinguishing differences
43.	FIRMAMENT	The expanse of the sky
44.	IMPREGNABLE	Unable to be captured, overthrown, or broken into
45.	LAMENTED	Expressed grief or regret; mourned
46.	NARY	Not any; no; never
47.	PERSECUTING	Pursuing with harassment; annoying persistently
48.	PRYING	Looking at closely or curiously
49.	SIDLED	Edged or moved up sideways
50.	TRANSGRESSIONS	Violations of laws or duties

Vocabulary Word Search - Go Ask Alice

```
M O N O P O L I Z E P H E N O M E N A J
D Q N P G L W S K J P R O D I G A L J W
J S N E R A M C C A R T I C U L A T E R
F N H R E M S F O R E B O D I N G L V V
M O J C G E K T N J G N I L F I T S A N
I I K E A N M W S F C P L C R C F C M X
N T T P R T G J C E B R R E Y N I K S
S I G T I E B W I M M S C P A L B N F M
C N T I O D S V E Z W R D V L S W T B X
R O B V U Q E Q N N I N H A Y H T E L Q
I M P E S S D S T M T O T P F L D R E B
P E R S E C U T I N G I S I E G E M A P
T R Y N X K E N O D N T T C C V G I R Y
I P I Z F E A I U G L N H Y H I E N Y Z
O D N R R T T S S Q N E Y F E N N A P L
N W G C I A M S L Y R T D I L D E B E H
D L S O L S N V R O A N D R O I R L N J
X I N E J I K A U R F O O M N C A E A L
D S V N A N N S O S F C L A M T T V N H
L E R D G I N I G H I Z C M U I E V C N
R F S M L N R N X V D S V E N V W Z E N
G I G V M E I K P F A M D N D E K W B V
D N Y L F V S B Z M V G L T A B L A S E
J K B N A H V D X Z I F R G N I M E E T
K R I R W F O R T I T U D E E W J V X T
```

AFFIDAVIT	DISCREET	INTERMINABLE	PRODIGAL
ARTICULATE	DISDAIN	LAMENTED	PRYING
ASININE	ECHELON	LECHEROUS	RAVINGS
ASTRAY	ENTITY	MONOPOLIZE	RECRIMINATIONS
BLASE	FINK	MUNDANE	REVELATION
BLEARY	FIRMAMENT	NARY	SIDLED
CLODDY	FOREBODING	PENANCE	SIEGE
CONCEIVE	FORTITUDE	PERCEPTIVE	STIFLING
CONSCIENTIOUS	GREGARIOUS	PERSECUTING	TEEMING
CONTENTION	INFERIOR	PHENOMENA	VACILLATING
DEGENERATE	INSCRIPTION	PREMONITIONS	VINDICTIVE

Answer Key Vocabulary Word Search - Go Ask Alice

AFFIDAVIT	DISCREET	INTERMINABLE	PRODIGAL
ARTICULATE	DISDAIN	LAMENTED	PRYING
ASININE	ECHELON	LECHEROUS	RAVINGS
ASTRAY	ENTITY	MONOPOLIZE	RECRIMINATIONS
BLASE	FINK	MUNDANE	REVELATION
BLEARY	FIRMAMENT	NARY	SIDLED
CLODDY	FOREBODING	PENANCE	SIEGE
CONCEIVE	FORTITUDE	PERCEPTIVE	STIFLING
CONSCIENTIOUS	GREGARIOUS	PERSECUTING	TEEMING
CONTENTION	INFERIOR	PHENOMENA	VACILLATING
DEGENERATE	INSCRIPTION	PREMONITIONS	VINDICTIVE

Vocabulary Crossword - Go Ask Alice

Across
1. Act of devotion to pay for a sin or wrongdoing
6. Stupid or of lesser dignity or value
9. Imagine; form an idea of
11. Seeking the company of others; outgoing and sociable
13. Informer, spy, or someone who squeals
15. Assault; attack
16. Bored with life or unimpressed
18. Full of things; swarming
19. Expressed grief or regret; mourned
20. The feeling that someone or something is unworthy of one's consideration or respect

Down
1. Looking at closely or curiously
2. Not any; no; never
3. In a way cooly unconcerned, indifferent, or casual
4. Level of command, authority, or rank
5. To have complete possession of; to dominate
7. Something that exists as its own self or being
8. Suggestive; lustful
10. Marking of words or a message on an item
12. Something that is uncovered, not previously known
14. Foolish; silly; stupid
17. Edged or moved up sideways

Answer Key Vocabulary Crossword - Go Ask Alice

				¹P	²E	N	³A	N	C	E				
⁴E		⁵M		R			N		O					
⁶C	L	O	D	D	Y		A		N		⁷E			⁸L
H		N		I			R		⁹C	O	N	C	¹⁰E	I	V	E
E		O		N			Y		H		T		N		C
L		P		¹¹G	¹²R	E	G	A	R	I	O	U	S		H
O		O			E				I		T		C		E
N		L			V				T		Y		R		R
	¹³F	I	N	K	E				A				I		O
¹⁴A		Z			L				N				P		U
¹⁵S	I	E	G	E	A		¹⁶B	L	A	¹⁷S	E		T		S
I					T					Y			I		
N		¹⁸T	E	E	M	I	N	G		I			O		
I					O					D			N		
N		¹⁹L	A	M	E	N	T	E	D					
E									²⁰D	I	S	D	A	I	N

Across
1. Act of devotion to pay for a sin or wrongdoing
6. Stupid or of lesser dignity or value
9. Imagine; form an idea of
11. Seeking the company of others; outgoing and sociable
13. Informer, spy, or someone who squeals
15. Assault; attack
16. Bored with life or unimpressed
18. Full of things; swarming
19. Expressed grief or regret; mourned
20. The feeling that someone or something is unworthy of one's consideration or respect

Down
1. Looking at closely or curiously
2. Not any; no; never
3. In a way cooly unconcerned, indifferent, or casual
4. Level of command, authority, or rank
5. To have complete possession of; to dominate
7. Something that exists as its own self or being
8. Suggestive; lustful
10. Marking of words or a message on an item
12. Something that is uncovered, not previously known
14. Foolish; silly; stupid
17. Edged or moved up sideways

Vocabulary Matching 1 - Go Ask Alice

___ 1. ASININE   A. Common; dull; boring; unimaginative

___ 2. FIRMAMENT   B. Advance warnings of the future

___ 3. MUNDANE   C. The expanse of the sky

___ 4. NONCHALANTLY   D. Off or away from the correct or right path

___ 5. PERCEPTIVE   E. Written statement or declaration made under oath

___ 6. INSCRIPTION   F. In a way cooly unconcerned, indifferent, or casual

___ 7. PREMONITIONS   G. Looking at closely or curiously

___ 8. PHENOMENA   H. Not any; no; never

___ 9. ENTITY   I. Pursuing with harassment; annoying persistently

___ 10. CONTENTION   J. Distinct, fluent, meaningful, and clear in the power of speech

___ 11. PRYING   K. Revengeful; with the desire to hurt another

___ 12. DISTINCTION   L. Understanding with insight or intuition

___ 13. FORTITUDE   M. Marking of words or a message on an item

___ 14. AFFIDAVIT   N. Disagreement; point of disagreement

___ 15. ASTRAY   O. To have complete possession of; to dominate

___ 16. NARY   P. Full of things; swarming

___ 17. PERSECUTING   Q. Suggestive; lustful

___ 18. MONOPOLIZE   R. Something that exists as its own self or being

___ 19. VINDICTIVE   S. Recognizing or distinguishing differences

___ 20. ARTICULATE   T. Foolish; silly; stupid

___ 21. TEEMING   U. Mental and emotional strength in facing difficulty

___ 22. REVELATION   V. Informer, spy, or someone who squeals

___ 23. FINK   W. Something that is remarkable, impressive, or extraordinary

___ 24. LECHEROUS   X. Something that is uncovered, not previously known

___ 25. ECHELON   Y. Level of command, authority, or rank

Answer Key Vocabulary Matching 1 - Go Ask Alice

T - 1.	ASININE	A. Common; dull; boring; unimaginative
C - 2.	FIRMAMENT	B. Advance warnings of the future
A - 3.	MUNDANE	C. The expanse of the sky
F - 4.	NONCHALANTLY	D. Off or away from the correct or right path
L - 5.	PERCEPTIVE	E. Written statement or declaration made under oath
M - 6.	INSCRIPTION	F. In a way cooly unconcerned, indifferent, or casual
B - 7.	PREMONITIONS	G. Looking at closely or curiously
W - 8.	PHENOMENA	H. Not any; no; never
R - 9.	ENTITY	I. Pursuing with harassment; annoying persistently
N - 10.	CONTENTION	J. Distinct, fluent, meaningful, and clear in the power of speech
G - 11.	PRYING	K. Revengeful; with the desire to hurt another
S - 12.	DISTINCTION	L. Understanding with insight or intuition
U - 13.	FORTITUDE	M. Marking of words or a message on an item
E - 14.	AFFIDAVIT	N. Disagreement; point of disagreement
D - 15.	ASTRAY	O. To have complete possession of; to dominate
H - 16.	NARY	P. Full of things; swarming
I - 17.	PERSECUTING	Q. Suggestive; lustful
O - 18.	MONOPOLIZE	R. Something that exists as its own self or being
K - 19.	VINDICTIVE	S. Recognizing or distinguishing differences
J - 20.	ARTICULATE	T. Foolish; silly; stupid
P - 21.	TEEMING	U. Mental and emotional strength in facing difficulty
X - 22.	REVELATION	V. Informer, spy, or someone who squeals
V - 23.	FINK	W. Something that is remarkable, impressive, or extraordinary
Q - 24.	LECHEROUS	X. Something that is uncovered, not previously known
Y - 25.	ECHELON	Y. Level of command, authority, or rank

Vocabulary Matching 2 - Go Ask Alice

___ 1. VINDICTIVE   A. Written statement or declaration made under oath
___ 2. ANTAGONISTIC   B. Expressed grief or regret; mourned
___ 3. CLODDY   C. Wild, delirious, or frenzied talking
___ 4. NONCHALANTLY   D. The feeling that someone or something is unworthy of one's consideration or respect
___ 5. LAMENTED   E. Indecisive; unsteady; wavering
___ 6. INFERIOR   F. Unending
___ 7. AFFIDAVIT   G. Informer, spy, or someone who squeals
___ 8. ASTRAY   H. Imagine; form an idea of
___ 9. TEEMING   I. Assault; attack
___10. VACILLATING   J. Not any; no; never
___11. SIEGE   K. Mental and emotional strength in facing difficulty
___12. NARY   L. Stupid or of lesser dignity or value
___13. RAVINGS   M. Disagreement; point of disagreement
___14. FINK   N. Unable to be captured, overthrown, or broken into
___15. FORTITUDE   O. Lengthy, formal speech or writing about a particular topic
___16. IMPREGNABLE   P. Seeking the company of others; outgoing and sociable
___17. DISTINCTION   Q. Off or away from the correct or right path
___18. CONSCIENTIOUS R. Revengeful; with the desire to hurt another
___19. CONCEIVE   S. In a way cooly unconcerned, indifferent, or casual
___20. GREGARIOUS   T. Lower in position, rank, or worth
___21. INTERMINABLE   U. Full of things; swarming
___22. DISDAIN   V. Hostile; unfriendly
___23. ARTICULATE   W. Recognizing or distinguishing differences
___24. CONTENTION   X. Distinct, fluent, meaningful, and clear in the power of speech
___25. DISSERTATION   Y. Characterized by taking extreme care and/or making great effort

Answer Key Vocabulary Matching 2 - Go Ask Alice

R - 1.	VINDICTIVE	A. Written statement or declaration made under oath
V - 2.	ANTAGONISTIC	B. Expressed grief or regret; mourned
L - 3.	CLODDY	C. Wild, delirious, or frenzied talking
S - 4.	NONCHALANTLY	D. The feeling that someone or something is unworthy of one's consideration or respect
B - 5.	LAMENTED	E. Indecisive; unsteady; wavering
T - 6.	INFERIOR	F. Unending
A - 7.	AFFIDAVIT	G. Informer, spy, or someone who squeals
Q - 8.	ASTRAY	H. Imagine; form an idea of
U - 9.	TEEMING	I. Assault; attack
E - 10.	VACILLATING	J. Not any; no; never
I - 11.	SIEGE	K. Mental and emotional strength in facing difficulty
J - 12.	NARY	L. Stupid or of lesser dignity or value
C - 13.	RAVINGS	M. Disagreement; point of disagreement
G - 14.	FINK	N. Unable to be captured, overthrown, or broken into
K - 15.	FORTITUDE	O. Lengthy, formal speech or writing about a particular topic
N - 16.	IMPREGNABLE	P. Seeking the company of others; outgoing and sociable
W - 17.	DISTINCTION	Q. Off or away from the correct or right path
Y - 18.	CONSCIENTIOUS	R. Revengeful; with the desire to hurt another
H - 19.	CONCEIVE	S. In a way cooly unconcerned, indifferent, or casual
P - 20.	GREGARIOUS	T. Lower in position, rank, or worth
F - 21.	INTERMINABLE	U. Full of things; swarming
D - 22.	DISDAIN	V. Hostile; unfriendly
X - 23.	ARTICULATE	W. Recognizing or distinguishing differences
M - 24.	CONTENTION	X. Distinct, fluent, meaningful, and clear in the power of speech
O - 25.	DISSERTATION	Y. Characterized by taking extreme care and/or making great effort

Vocabulary Juggle Letters 1 - Go Ask Alice

1. SRVIGNA = 1. _____
   Wild, delirious, or frenzied talking

2. TMNAICENRIROSI = 2. _____
   Accusations in response to accusations from someone else

3. YRAN = 3. _____
   Not any; no; never

4. ARENEGTDEE = 4. _____
   One who falls below the desirable level of quality

5. NIYTET = 5. _____
   Something that exists as its own self or being

6. KFNI = 6. _____
   Informer, spy, or someone who squeals

7. LDYDOC = 7. _____
   Stupid or of lesser dignity or value

8. OZNIMELPOO = 8. _____
   To have complete possession of; to dominate

9. OCNYLNLTAHAN = 9. _____
   In a way cooly unconcerned, indifferent, or casual

10. TNISONMOREIP =10. _____
    Advance warnings of the future

11. NAAICNGITTOS =11. _____
    Hostile; unfriendly

12. GENTEIM =12. _____
    Full of things; swarming

13. GROUGARESI =13. _____
    Seeking the company of others; outgoing and sociable

14. ATISGSONRRSSNE =14. _____
    Violations of laws or duties

15. NEFOIIRR =15. _____
    Lower in position, rank, or worth

Answer Key Vocabulary Juggle Letters 1 - Go Ask Alice

1. SRVIGNA = 1. RAVINGS
   Wild, delirious, or frenzied talking

2. TMNAICENRIROSI = 2. RECRIMINATIONS
   Accusations in response to accusations from someone else

3. YRAN = 3. NARY
   Not any; no; never

4. ARENEGTDEE = 4. DEGENERATE
   One who falls below the desirable level of quality

5. NIYTET = 5. ENTITY
   Something that exists as its own self or being

6. KFNI = 6. FINK
   Informer, spy, or someone who squeals

7. LDYDOC = 7. CLODDY
   Stupid or of lesser dignity or value

8. OZNIMELPOO = 8. MONOPOLIZE
   To have complete possession of; to dominate

9. OCNYLNLTAHAN = 9. NONCHALANTLY
   In a way cooly unconcerned, indifferent, or casual

10. TNISONMOREIP =10. PREMONITIONS
    Advance warnings of the future

11. NAAICNGITTOS =11. ANTAGONISTIC
    Hostile; unfriendly

12. GENTEIM =12. TEEMING
    Full of things; swarming

13. GROUGARESI =13. GREGARIOUS
    Seeking the company of others; outgoing and sociable

14. ATISGSONRRSSNE =14. TRANSGRESSIONS
    Violations of laws or duties

15. NEFOIIRR =15. INFERIOR
    Lower in position, rank, or worth

Vocabulary Juggle Letters 2 - Go Ask Alice

1. IVDEVCIINT = 1. _____
   Revengeful; with the desire to hurt another

2. TVPICREPEE = 2. _____
   Understanding with insight or intuition

3. IAOSERGGRU = 3. _____
   Seeking the company of others; outgoing and sociable

4. GILFNTSI = 4. _____
   Smothering or suffocating

5. NRGPYI = 5. _____
   Looking at closely or curiously

6. EBRINGFOOD = 6. _____
   Strong feeling of coming misfortune or evil

7. YCDODL = 7. _____
   Stupid or of lesser dignity or value

8. SSTSNRSGNOIAER = 8. _____
   Violations of laws or duties

9. YTNIET = 9. _____
   Something that exists as its own self or being

10. GSIRVNA = 10. _____
    Wild, delirious, or frenzied talking

11. AIVIGLNTACL = 11. _____
    Indecisive; unsteady; wavering

12. OSEHLCURE = 12. _____
    Suggestive; lustful

13. SECTIOIUCNNOS = 13. _____
    Characterized by taking extreme care and/or making great effort

14. IOOMPOEZLN = 14. _____
    To have complete possession of; to dominate

15. NCGASOATITIN = 15. _____
    Hostile; unfriendly

Answer Key Vocabulary Juggle Letters 2 - Go Ask Alice

1. IVDEVCIINT = 1. VINDICTIVE
Revengeful; with the desire to hurt another

2. TVPICREPEE = 2. PERCEPTIVE
Understanding with insight or intuition

3. IAOSERGGRU = 3. GREGARIOUS
Seeking the company of others; outgoing and sociable

4. GILFNTSI = 4. STIFLING
Smothering or suffocating

5. NRGPYI = 5. PRYING
Looking at closely or curiously

6. EBRINGFOOD = 6. FOREBODING
Strong feeling of coming misfortune or evil

7. YCDODL = 7. CLODDY
Stupid or of lesser dignity or value

8. SSTSNRSGNOIAER = 8. TRANSGRESSIONS
Violations of laws or duties

9. YTNIET = 9. ENTITY
Something that exists as its own self or being

10. GSIRVNA =10. RAVINGS
Wild, delirious, or frenzied talking

11. AIVIGLNTACL =11. VACILLATING
Indecisive; unsteady; wavering

12. OSEHLCURE =12. LECHEROUS
Suggestive; lustful

13. SECTIOIUCNNOS =13. CONSCIENTIOUS
Characterized by taking extreme care and/or making great effort

14. IOOMPOEZLN =14. MONOPOLIZE
To have complete possession of; to dominate

15. NCGASOATITIN =15. ANTAGONISTIC
Hostile; unfriendly

www.ingramcontent.com/pod-product-compliance
Lightning Source LLC
Chambersburg PA
CBHW051408070526
44584CB00023B/3345